A
McCormic
Project

CHASE R. HOLLIE

ISBN 978-1-0980-3546-4 (paperback)
ISBN 978-1-0980-3547-1 (digital)

Christian Faith Publishing, Inc.
832 Park Avenue
Meadville, PA 16335
www.christianfaithpublishing.com

Printed in the United States of America

CHAPTER ONE

It's been a long day, emotions all over the place, and not once did time ever stand as still as it stood at this moment right now. Sitting here in my study with the fireplace lit, listening to an old record spinning on the old record player I had purchased at a flea market while I was in college. Thumbing through this photo album and drowning my sorrows in this bottle of spirits. I know drinking doesn't solve anything, but I needed something to drown out the noisy thoughts in my head. I was reliving every memory on every page until I came to this very photo. My desk was overwhelmed with a clutter of photos as well, but this photo captured my attention.

The photo that caught my attention was an old photograph featuring a woman I had met a little while ago that would change things in my life, Kira Alexander. The year I met Kira marked an unforgettable turning point in my life. I had met Kira years ago at a local high school football game. It was a cold crowded October night. It was a traditional event. A night out of the season where two of the town's historic high school rivals were going head to head for redemption or possible bragging rights for the new season. That night, I was scooting and weaving through rows of students and laps of locals cheering for their teenagers or old high school alma mater. After a thousand "pardon me" and a million times of saying "excuse me," I had finally worked my way to a small vacant seat in the center of the crowd.

"My heavens, it sure is cold tonight," I heard the lady sitting next to me mumble. To my left was a woman shivering with her arms folded tightly and hands tucked in her under arms.

Though she wasn't talking to me, I made a reply to her comment. "Yes, it sure is. Thousands of us locals do this every year. Every year we look forward to this breath freezing night. We all bundle up in the warmest clothing we can find in the farthest corners of our homes. On this very night, we come out here and cheer on our sons, daughters, and old alma maters. You can say that it's a bit of a home town tradition." It was a tradition dating back to when the second high school had been built. You are witnessing a harmless event, overflowing with competitive teenage spirits colliding throughout the transition of adolescence to adulthood. Majority of the people that attend this event have either, attended one of the two high schools and passed down the so-called "grudge" to their children. We all took it a bit too serious as teenagers, but as we got older, the inner hatred faded. Although some may never grow out of it, most of the community continues to be passionate about the win loss record between the rivals. It was good, old-fashioned hatred, but nothing harmful ever came from it.

"Oh no, not me, I'm a spring and summer girl myself. I'm just in town to watch my niece. She is the captain of the cheerleading squad for the home team. She has been writing and calling me for months. I have been promising to come see her cheer for as long as she has been asking. She and I are pretty close. You could say we are like best friends. Ever since I can remember, we have spent our summers together. Every summer I come in for a weekend and she comes back home with me to gossip, go shopping, and watch movies. All while eating everything that goes against my diet." She replied with a grin, pointing toward the cheerleader closest to the stands at the center of the formation. "There she is, the short brunette in the front of the formation. She may be the smallest out the bunch but she carries the spirit of the pack. I am so proud of her." Her niece waived at her as she was pointing toward her. I had thought to myself; the girl's mother and her must share a strong resemblance because the child looks very much like her aunt.

"I bet she sure is something. She resembles you quite a bit. She seems passionate about what she does. It's an honor to be a captain or a leader of any team or particular group. I bet her parents sure are proud as well."

"Yes, they would have been. She lost them when she was five months old if I can recall. They were on their anniversary cruise when the ship sank. They were amongst some of the unfortunate members who weren't rescued in time." Just when you feel like you are giving a good compliment, it's always a sad story to follow that makes you feel like you are sticking your foot in your mouth. I hate it that the child lost her parents. I hate it for any child to be deprived the opportunity of two loving parents. Even though in today's world we have split households or households with both parents, in which one nor the other are involved in the child's life.

"Oh my, that sounds tragic. Here, take this blanket. Hopefully it will keep you warm. I always bring a spare just in case. Perhaps some homemade hot cocoa would knock the chill off those lips?" Poor thing sure was shivering. You could tell she was cold as her teeth started to chatter during our conversation.

"Thank you! Yes, some cocoa would be nice," she replied while wrapping herself tightly in the blanket as she smiled and shivered.

"Then hot cocoa it is. I will go and bring you some back from the concession stand." I got up and wrestled my way back through the crowd, making my way down to the concession stand. Wow, she sure is beautiful, I thought to myself as I got in line to make my order. The line isn't as long as I thought it would be. I should be back in no time. I think I should grab a few extra snacks in case she might be a little hungry.

"Miss me?" I said sarcastically. "I picked up a few extra snacks in case you got the munchies. It won't satisfy any hunger but it may alleviate the appetite for the time being."

"Thank you very much! I was a bit hungry". She tucked her hair behind her ears with her index finger, then took a sip of cocoa.

"By the way, my name is Kyle, Kyle McCormic. How rude of me not to introduce myself, sitting here babbling on as a total stranger." I took out a napkin and wiped the salt of the popcorn from my fingertips as I extended my hand.

"Kira, Kira Alexander," she replied as she accepted my gesture.

She was a beautiful brunette. I couldn't help but to notice her pretty blue eyes. I have always personally thought a woman having dark hair and light eyes a rare combination. Her hands were soft as cotton. I was immediately apprehended by her voice and smile. A part of me wants to pursue her further. I bet she has some stud waiting for her back home. Should I ask for her number, email, home address, or some sort of way I can keep in touch with her? Who knows? I'm not much of a ladies man or a bee charmer, but I would hate for this night to end without the assurance of whether or not I will see her again. I knew she said that she had come to see her niece cheer, but I could tell that she had lost interest in the festivities. Plus, the deficit in the score between the two teams is so far spread that it is more than obvious what the outcome of this year's game is going to be. I don't think there would be any harm in asking her out for coffee.

"Well, Ms. Alexander, the game is almost over. I'm sure by looking at this score; we can pretty much predict the outcome of this showdown. Would you like to join me for a cup of coffee later? Not at my house of course, it would be a public place." My, that was hard. I have never been the one to ask a woman on a date, to hang out, or anything. It always made me feel weird. I wasn't one for rejection. I was always afraid that the woman would feel like I had some cruel intention or would look at me like some pervert. Maybe it has always been a lack of confidence or me just being silly. Then again, you just don't know with all these creeps and weirdoes these days. I don't date much and it's not like I do something like this on the regular. If she lived in town then I know that I would have a better chance of seeing her again and then asking, but I figure I'd better make my move now or lose out on what could be a good opportunity.

"Sure, that would be nice. I wasn't going to do much but go back to my parents and go to bed. I'm sure my niece has plans to hang out with her friends after the game tonight anyway. She and I have plans for breakfast in the morning. So I don't believe I am breaking any arrangements. Coffee and some chit-chat, does sound nice. Is there a place that you have in mind? Somewhere I can meet you because I drove my own car, and I would hate to leave it here."

"Actually there is a nice little coffee shop not too far from here, Alice's Café. It's a small coffee shop on the corner of Walsh and Elkhart. I can meet you there in about twenty or thirty minutes from now?" I bet she stands me up. She probably thinks I'm awful strange to ask a girl I just met out for coffee; either strange, desperate, or some kidnapping rapist. I bet she doesn't show.

"Thirty minutes sounds efficient enough by looking at this crowd and estimating how long it will take for either one of us to get out of here."

I guess she may be a little interested in going, but I bet she stands me up. "I'll meet you there in thirty then."

She seems like a nice gal. She gives off the vibe of being a bit down to earth. Maybe the down home type or as my mother would say "Ole Plain Jane" by her not wearing a lot of make up or if none at all. Not that she needed it or anything. I had always felt women that wore lots of make-up had something to hide. I found her strikingly gorgeous without it. She has a bit of our hometown accent. I could tell that most of it has faded away over the time she has been gone. She carries the demeanor of someone who may work at a doctor's office or a woman in the medical field. Listen to yourself Kyle, babbling on like you are about to propose. It's just coffee!

I love Alice's Café! It has been a part of this community since before I was even thought of. It's a family business inherited by many generations in the Brown family. I can remember coming here every Saturday morning for milk, apple pie, and to collect my thoughts. To me, it was like my own place of peace with familiar faces and all the elders treating me as though I am their own son.

The brass bell caught my attention as the door opened. I looked over my shoulder and there she was shaking off the cold from outside. As she overlooked the place, I threw my hand up to let her know I was here.

"This is a nice place. I like it. Do you come here often?" she asked as she sat down into the small booth.

"Actually, I have been a bit of a slacker here lately. I usually come every Saturday. I have been coming here ever since I was allowed ride my bike around town. I am a regular here. Everyone knows me. Even this booth is like my own personal spot. If you look up to your right, there is a picture of me when I was a kid. That's me, the one sipping the milkshake. Mrs. Brown placed it there to mark this booth once she noticed how much of a regular I had become."

"Cute. So I take it that you are the hometown boy that everyone knows and loves?"

"I wouldn't call it that, but I have been around a while. My face is pretty familiar. Ever since I can remember, I have always had a knack for people. My father used to take me to the local barber shop and to all of his friend's houses. I would spend time soaking up knowledge from the older generations past experiences. I would often ride my bike to visit my mother at work. She was employed by the local nursing home. I would only go for a few hours. A lot of the times I would stay and help with most of the recreational activities." I hope I'm not boring her to death talking about me. I'm sure she would hate to spend her night listening to some man rant on and on about his hometown history.

"So, Ms. Alexander, tell me about your history in this town before you decided to fly the nest? Tell me why we never crossed paths when we were children or as teenagers?"

"My sister and I were close and somewhat sheltered. We attended a private academy up state. Our parents wanted us to focus more on our future. They figured shipping us off to what they called the finest schools would help us do just that. Ever since my sister and I attended such schools and college, we only came in on some week-ends and a few of the holidays."

As she told me this story, I couldn't help but notice that she never took her eyes off the menu. Maybe it's nothing to really pay attention to. Some people just aren't into looking the other person in the eyes or face during conversation, shy type I reckon. Then again she may not be all that interested in me. Plus she does seem well groomed and pretty smart, so I guess I could believe the upstate school bit.

"Academics, private schools, and colleges—sounds like you and your sister were fortunate to receive a wonderful education. Maybe I know your parents. What is it that they do for a living?"

"No, you wouldn't. My parents live off my father's inheritance. They are quite the antisocial couple. Few friends and enough money to keep them company. They live in the suburbs on the outskirts of town. Business, business, and more business, that's all they know. Anyway, what is it that you do Mr. McCormic, the hometown golden boy?" I take it that she was mocking me with that question, being that she smiled and quoted it with her fingers.

"Well, I grew up to become the head director and recreational coordinator for the local nursing home my mother used to work for. Hopefully someday I will own my own."

"Darling, I'm sure you have stared at that menu long enough. Are you ready to order?" the waitress interrupted me with sarcasm in her voice and a smile on her face as she spoke to Kira, then winked and smiled at me.

"Yes, ma'am. I'm not really all that hungry. I will have the strawberry milkshake with two strawberries on top, and two straws."

"And what will you be eating tonight, Mr. McCormic?"

"I will have a slice of caramel cheesecake and a glass of water. Thank you, Rachel!"

"You're welcome. Your orders will be out in a few minutes." She folded up her pin and pad, tucked it under her arm, took our menus, and strutted off to the kitchen.

"Rachel, Mr. McCormic, plus you got a wink and a smile. Is there anything that I don't know about? Hopefully she is not an old flame and I just happen to be sitting in the wrong seat. Do you bring all your girls her?" Kira asked sarcastically.

"No not at all. Actually, Rachel is a little older than me and she used to be my sitter when I was a kid. Even before then, her mother would sit for my parents when they were children. Now as I think of it, I have known Rachel all my life. I guess just saying that would have been easier than giving you the "baby sitter rundown." She is one of my closest friends, if not like my sister. If you ever come here with me again in the future, you will notice that they all are quite nice to me. I have either known them since I was a child or one of their relatives may be a resident at the nursing home. That wink and smile she gave me was probably because I am usually alone when I come here."

"Again, are you planning on seeing me again?"

Rachel had returned with our orders. She silently placed Kira's strawberry shake in front of her, my cheesecake and water in front of me, then, proceeded with the rest of the customers.

"You seem to be an interesting person, and I mean that in a good way. Maybe after the night is over you may find it okay to keep in touch? If not, then I hope by some chance I will see you again." She smiled at the comment, but something tells me that I am in for a challenge. Men always have to be the predator, and as for the prey; it's their decision on whether they will be captured in the hunt. Truly, I would love to get to know her more and see her on some sort of a date in the future. I consider myself lucky tonight. I'm not much of an impromptu person.

As I indulged in my cheesecake and she sipped her milkshake, there was never a dull moment in our conversation. I could tell she was getting a little more comfortable with the stranger she had met at the football game. I reckon I didn't do too badly for my one of few times asking a female out. I was really having a good time. It was nice to hear her stories of college and career. The more she sipped, the less shake she had to finish. On a night like this, I wish the glasses at the coffee shop were a bit bigger.

"Well, Mr. McCormic, the shake was delicious. I must say that it was nice meeting you but I should be going. Chelsie and I have a big day ahead of us tomorrow. You know how it is when we girls get together. There isn't enough time in a day to get done with all of the things we set out to accomplish! Hopefully I will see you again soon." She stood up, smiled, and extended her hand.

"Well, if that is the case, then your number or some way to reach you would be nice?" I asked.

"I like to leave things to fate, with enough hope," she replied.

"Then hopefully we will cross paths again!" I smiled as I stood up to shake her hand and help her with her coat.

"Good night, Mr. McComic." She smiled then turned and walked out of the restaurant. Her smile lingered in my mind for the rest of the night. As I drove home, I thought it clever of her to place this stain on my mind and to leave herself lingering in my thoughts. Before I go home, I think I should stop by and check in with the fellas over at the "Hole in the Wall." Maybe they have heard of a Kira Alexander, or remember her and her sister?

The Hole in the Wall is a locally owned sports bar that the guys and I normally go to hang out on game nights. Often on game nights, the fellas and I go out to enjoy sports, burgers, and wings. Not to mention, the female selection of sports fans aren't that bad to look at as well. As I entered through the door, the bar was crowded. I could see Marcus and Trent sitting in the far back corner. As I arrived at the table I began to take off my coat and drape it over the chair next to me.

"How is the action tonight fellas?" I asked as we all shook hands before I took my seat.

"Terrible, I'm losing the college football pool we have going on at work. This is just not my weekend, bro," Trent replied. "Although, by the looks of the bar, there are plenty of the town's best to be recruited." Trenton Lacy, sports fanatic-slash-lady's man, but not really. He isn't quite the power hitter at the plate when it comes to the ladies. More strike outs than base hits, but hey, he's always on deck. He runs his mother's family business on the south side. "Lacy's Living Room" the most successful furniture store in town. I've known Trent all my life, from the sandbox to present day. He and I even attended college together.

"Yeah, my team isn't doing so hot themselves. How about you? How is your night turning out? Did the Vikings win tonight?" Marcus chimed in. Marcus McCormic, former Highland High School star quarterback, the town's athletic hero. He was at one time one of the nation's best in football. He had a pretty decent college career and went on to play two seasons of professional football before he was in a car accident that injured his shoulder of his throwing arm. After his career ended, he came back home and is now a foreman for his father's construction company. He and I are first cousins. His father is my father's brother.

"The Vikings suck this year. That new coach and coaching staff better plan a short career here and look forward to new jobs somewhere else. You guys know that this town and the parents will not stand for the town's oldest high school standing to take a beating like they did tonight. I don't see them getting through the first round of the playoffs, let alone hanging another state championship banner this year." We all attended Highland High School as teenagers. It was every kid's dream to attend or play football and basketball for the Highland Vikings. They always went deep in the playoffs. It was guaranteed that one out of four years of your attendance, they would win the state championship, and the school would let out for the week of the championship. "Any of you two remember a girl named Kira Alexander, fairly beautiful, dark hair, blue eyes, and about average height?"

"Hey, boys, hope I'm not interrupting the guy's night of sports and women!" We were interrupted by our life-long female sidekick Julia Ann Cowan, wrapping her arms around Marcus's neck from behind with a kiss on his cheek. "Jacs" is what we called her. It was the nickname she was given by my mother. No matter what the guys and I were doing, Jacs was always right there in the mix. Jacs was, and always will be known as the town's biggest tomboy. She was outstanding in soccer, softball, basketball, and track. Heck, she even kicked field goals for the varsity football team in high school. She became a sports therapist at the town's hospital. She was like our little sister growing up. She never approved of any girl that either of us ever dated and never was afraid to tell the girls that we were dating. After high school, she went on to attend college out west on a full-ride athletic scholarship in softball. Still, we all maintained contact and would get together during the holidays. Even in college, we would spend our breaks together on some sort of planned trip. She and Marcus have been engaged to be married for going on two years. Their wedding is three weekends from now. They didn't become an item until Marcus had come home after the accident. You could always tell they had a thing for each other back in high school. They just never got around to calling themselves a couple. They ended up attending separate colleges in college. Along with his rehabilitation, she helped him through his depression after losing his football career. I guess you could say it's possible to lose a love of something and gain a better one somewhere else. No matter what, I will always say that it worked out for the good of the both of them. It brought them together and they have a beautiful relationship that anyone in the world could be envious of, including me.

"No, bro, I don't recall any Kira Alexander," Trent replied.

"Me neither. How about you, honey? Do you recall a Kira Alexander back when we were in high school?" Marcus turned and asked Jacs.

"No, I can't say that name is stored anywhere in my memory bank as well," Jacs replied, shaking her head as she answered the question. "Did she attend Highland or Prep?"

"She says she and her sister were sent to a private school throughout their childhood and teenage years." This is an intriguing situation. None of us have ever heard of this girl and her sister. Surely all of us would have crossed paths somewhere in this town. "The Alexanders are her parents. Do any of you recall the Alexanders having any children?"

"The Alexanders—that rich and stuck-up Alexander family that live in that big house in the suburbs on the outskirts of town? My, my, Kyle, you really are swinging for the fence bro. Trying to make it to the big leagues, hey?" Marcus replied with laughter and sarcasm in his voice. "At first it sounds like a wild goose chase, but turns out it's a treasure hunt instead."

"I could care less about the money," I calmly replied, starring off into the bar. "Aside from the mysterious fact that neither of us have ever heard of her or her sister—she is absolutely beautiful. I met her at the game tonight. I bought her cocoa. We chatted for a bit. Then I invited her to Alice's for coffee and more chitchat. Heck, I even loaned her my blanket that Mom had made out of our old athletic sweat shirts. Darn it!" I yelled as I quietly pounded my fist on the table. "She still has my blanket. She never gave it back." That blanket meant a lot to me.

"Wow, I am anxious to meet her," Jacs chimed in, head up, eyes wide open, with her chest stuck out. "She must have really been beautiful for a man to show such chivalry. It's hard to keep your cousin over here from snatching off all the cover while we sleep. To get a beverage and a blanket from him while he is up is like pulling teeth."

"Whelp, that's our cue, fellas. I think it's time we called it a night babe. We all have had a long night and all of us have to get up for work in the a.m. I reckon, I'll go home and work on sharing some cover or just bringing a spare blanket to the bedroom, huh?" Marcus smiled, teasing Jacs as he put on his coat, and then helping Jacs with hers. "Seriously, if she is truly interested in you, cousin, she will return that blanket. Trust me, like we always say, 'All things happen for a reason.' That blanket is your dog in the fight and it my friend, will lead our mystery woman back to you," Marcus added as he and Jacs were starting away from the table out of the bar. Trent and I followed them outside to the parking lot.

Trent patted me on the shoulder before getting into his car. He rolled down his window and said, "He is right. I wouldn't worry too much about it Cinderella. Your princess has your glass slipper!" Laughing as he drove off.

As I drove home, I thought about meeting Kira and if I would ever see her again. I sure hope the fellas were right about her returning the blanket.

CHAPTER TWO

While I was driving to work today, I was thinking to myself a week had gone by and no word from a Kira Alexander. Her smile that night at the high school game and diner replay in my mind a million times a day. I wonder if she was just pulling my leg with that whole fate and hope speech? I called myself doing a little research at the nursing home. I asked a few nurses if they knew anything of Kira or anything about the Alexanders. One thing that did match up with Kira's story is that her mother and father did have a boat load of money and lived on the outskirts of town, but none of them could place Kira's name with her face. Also, no one could recall the Alexanders having any children. Maybe it would be wise to ask one of the residents, but then again, I don't think they would be much help with knowing her. I guess if I want to find out anything, I would have to ask Kira. Laughing to myself, I thought of going to the Alexanders and just asking them their family history.

As I entered the nursing home, there she was at the front desk. I could only see her from a distance. One way I was sure that it was her is because I recognized the blanket that I had given her the night of the game. She had it folded and draped over her left arm. She turned, smiled, and waved, then began to approach as the reception-ist pointed toward me coming through the door.

"Hello, Kira. What brings you to the nursing home today?" I acted as though I hadn't even noticed the blanket. I hope that the borrowed blanket isn't the only reason she had to find me. With her hair being pulled back, I could get the full view of her face in a bet-ter light. She hasn't been in my presence for five minutes, and I am already sucked into those pretty ocean blue eyes, full lips, and sweet smile. Her choice of fashion once again wasn't anything too fancy. She was wearing a black wool pea coat, gray hooded sweat shirt, jeans, and tennis shoes.

"I was cleaning out my car the other day. I found this blanket in the back seat. As I looked over all the material on it, I figured you might want it back. So here I am to return it to you. Thank you for letting me borrow it that night. I was really cold that night!" The innocence in her eyes could stop a charging bull in his tracks. Although, I could care less about the blanket, I'm glad something reminded her of me while she was away. Because I could not stop thinking about her since the night we meet. It wasn't because no one could recall her ever living or going to school in town, but because I was seriously attracted to this woman. Somehow I feel like we made a strong connection that night.

"Fate." I smiled with a little volume in my voice. I had to think fast before she walked out of my life again without taking another shot at getting better acquainted. "I remember you said that you would like to leave things to fate or hope. Being that this blanket brought you to me. Would it be wrong of me to entitle you to your words that night at the diner? You did say, and I quote, "I like to leave things up to fate and hope." If I must, I would consider this pretty darn close," as I acknowledged the blanket tucked under my left arm. "How about we grab a bite to eat later this afternoon when I get off? I know a place in town where the food is mouth-watering. You interested?"

"I did say fate. Being that you quoted me so well, and seemingly holding me accountable to my own words. I guess I owe you this afternoon," as she smiled back, slightly rocking back and forth.

"I get off at four. How does five sound? I will meet you back here. I only live ten minutes away from here. I can get cleaned up real fast and meet you back here in the parking lot. We can go out for a bite to eat?"

"Five sounds good to me. I will see you at five." She smiled, shook my hand, and started back down the hall. I stood there for a moment, watching her as she walked out the door. She doesn't carry herself as though her family is loaded with money. Something about her seems simple, common, nothing from wealth. I could smell her scent on the blanket as I refolded it and tucked it up under my arm. I can't really tell if she is interested in me or not. Maybe she just sees this as a new friendship. I hope it's because she is just taking her time getting to know me. I must say that I really am attracted to her. Hopefully today goes by fast and comes to a halt at five o'clock.

I had constantly checked my watch all day long waiting for four o'clock. I even took on extra task today to pass the time. I must say that even my lunch break took longer than usual. It's funny how time slows itself when you are anxiously awaiting a special appointment.

"Four is finally here and I sure as heck won't be staying late today. I am on my way home to get cleaned up Mrs. Sharon."

"You have a good night tonight Mr. McCormic," replied the receptionist. Mrs. Sharon had been a receptionist at the nursing home for years. I remember her working the front desk when I was a little boy on the days I would come in and volunteer to help. Every morning, she would have her coffee and be reading the newspaper. Funny thing that I will always remember about Mrs. Sharon is that she wore prescription eye glasses but always looked over the top of them when she read the paper or any form of literature of the matter. "The girl that came to visit you today sure was pretty. I don't reckon I have seen her around these parts before, outta towner?"

"Actually she is from here, Kira Alexander is her name. Her parents are the Alexander couple that live in the suburbs on the out-skirts of town." After I said that, I was extremely curious to how Mrs. Sharon would respond, being that no one recalls the Alexanders having any children. She looked up and off from her computer screen, squinting her eyes, as though she was searching her life long memory bank. Then she replied with a peculiar look on her face.

"The Alexanders, I didn't know they had any children. Then again, it wasn't like they were a part of any social group in this town. Rarely do you ever see Mr. Alexander here in town, unless it's at the bank or the local drugstore to pick up meds for Mrs. Alexander."

"Well, that's who she said her parents were. I'm off, see you tomorrow," waving as I left.

As I drove home I couldn't help but to think it strange that no one can recall a Kira Alexander or the Alexanders having any children. It may be because the Alexander family isn't originally from here. Kira and her sister may have already been in private school during the time the family moved to town. Surely they had to come home for the summer. I will give her some time to open up before I ask such an intriguing question. It is hard to ignore the curiosity or strangeness of the situation, because it seems such a mystery that no one knows this girl claiming to be a daughter to a couple that no one remembers having any children. Who am I to think wrong or judge anyone? It isn't like I came from the laps of luxury or never had past moments in my life that I would love to erase. Hmm, what to wear? Nothing too casual, she doesn't come off as the flashy type. So I'm sure she won't be wearing anything elegant. I'm sure I won't be over dressed by wearing a casual sweater, jeans, and my boots. I took a quick shower, got dressed, and dashed out the door. As I pulled into the nursing home parking lot, I could see the lights of Kira's car pulling in behind me. She parked her car in the space beside mine, got out, and started around the front of the vehicle over to the passenger side.

"Well, aren't I glad to see you Ms. Alexander," smiling sarcastically as she opened the door and sat down in the passenger seat.

"Oh, a man with a sense of humor, that's cool, I can dig it," laughing as she got into the car. "So where is this so-called nice place you plan on taking me?"

"Just relax and enjoy the night. Let me do the driving and trust that no matter where we go, you are in good hands. How have you been since I've seen you last?"

"I have been doing quite well, business has been good. Just the other day, I had a few clients cancel some appointments, because they will be going on their annual vacation. I saw it as an opportunity for a vacation for myself as well. So I packed up, came home to see my parents, and my niece for a few days. As I was throwing my bags in the car, I noticed the blanket and remembered that I had also planned on returning it to you as well. Are you glad I returned it?"

"Yes, but I will admit that it isn't the blanket that I am glad to see return. It's who returned with it that concerns me more than the blanket itself. I'm glad it brought you back to me. I guess I need to devise a plan to get you to return to me more often." Okay, I couldn't wait any longer. I may as well be upfront and let her know that I am interested in her. Hopefully she can catch the hint off that alone. I don't think it could be spelled out more plainly than that.

"You wouldn't be getting sweet on me now, would you, Mr. McCormic?" I noticed the giggle in her voice as she replied to the comment.

"If I were, would it save me all the trouble of trying to scheme up ways of getting you back in town?"

"No, Kyle, no scheme necessary; I plan on moving back to town this spring. My parents are getting old and it would allow me to help more with my niece. I will be taking a teaching job at the high school, and hopefully somewhere in my spare time I can write my book."

"Book, you're a writer?" I asked surprisingly.

"No, I am actually a personal trainer at the gym in the town I live in. I originally went to college and finished to become a teacher. I had gotten board during my summer breaks, so I had gotten my personal trainers license to pass the time. I guess you could say that I had taken quite a bit of interest in physical fitness, and put teaching on the shelf for a little while. I'm no book writer by far, but I used to love to write short stories when I was a little girl. I always wondered if I could ever write a book that may become a bestseller and turn into a movie someday. I love my career as a personal trainer, but I think it would be nice to explore my talents in writing as well."

"Versatility, I like that. It's always good to have options and have a career in something you are truly interested in. Should I get somewhat excited that you are moving back into town? Hopefully that will allow me to see you more?" Once again, there it is, honey, my intentions laid out there for you to pick up and approve. I feel like we are playing a game of poker and I just showed her my cards with all my chips on the table.

"I would say that would be a reason for you and me both to be excited. I think it would be a great opportunity for us to spend more time together. Plus, I think I have fallen in love with Alice's Cafe," smiling as she commented. Heck, before she said Alice's Café, I was sure was going to say that she had fallen in love with me. Doesn't matter, got to start somewhere; may as well be from scratch.

"Well, I look forward to our future relationship, whatever it may become, and make sure that my book is the first one that you autograph!"

"I promise!" she replied.

"Well, here we are. I hope you like Italian. I, myself, am a sucker for Alfredo and this place has the best chicken and shrimp Alfredo that I have ever put in my mouth." I really do hope she likes Italian because I know that I didn't even bother to ask her if she had a preference of food origin.

"Italian is fine. I'm really not a picky eater." I opened the door for her as we entered the restaurant. The host greeted us and led us to our table. He removed Kira's coat, placed it on the back of her chair, and seated her at the table. Gazing at her as she studied the menu carefully, I had begun to thinking to myself. Casual sweater, slacks, and heels—sophisticated but once again, not too dressy. The fellas and I were used to going for the glamour girls but Jacs always ran them off. I think it was because she knew that whoever we would end up marrying, she would have to get along with and she could never fit in with those types. Having a girl with a personality similar to Jacs doesn't seem all that bad any way. I have known Jacs for forever. I would honestly say that she is probably one of the best women I know. Over the years, I have realized that I have judged every date to the approval of my mother, or Jacs. The waiter had finally arrived at our table to take our orders.

"What, will you two be having this evening?" he asked.

"I will have a glass of water and the shrimp and chicken alfredo. And what would you like for dinner, Kira?"

She folded her menu, looked up at the waiter, smiled, and then proceeded to order. "Make that two glasses of water, and is it possible to order a big bowl of that Alfredo with two forks?" I was impressed with her request. Never in my experience of dating have I heard of such a request. I was totally caught off guard, but I really liked the way she had ordered.

"Yes, ma'am, I am sure that I can arrange for that somehow. I will be back with your order in a moment." The waiter took up our menus and proceeded to the kitchen to place our orders.

"Wow, are you an alfredo lover as well?" Laughing as I acknowledged the order that she had placed.

"I like alfredo, but you did say it was the best. I guess I figured I would try it as well. Are you not the sharing kind, Mr. McCormic?"

"Oh, I don't mind at all. You are just the first woman that I have ever been out with that has done anything like that. Not that I'm not impressed, because I am." I really like this girl and I think that she will be a hard case for Jacs to crack. Actually, I think that Jacs will approve of this one and my mother will be delighted to meet her.

The night went on as we shared conversation and alfredo. Not once did she mention anything about her family except for her plans to get her own place, and for her niece to come stay with her until she finishes high school to go off to college. By the way she talks about her niece, I could tell they had a special bond, and deep love for one another. Though the child had lost her parents at an early age and to have no memories of them, I could say that having Kira as a replacement was a true blessing. I was truly enjoying myself and hoping the night wouldn't end, but time had sped up. I noticed how it was moving faster than it was while I was at work earlier today. Before the night is over, I am going to ask her to be my date for the wedding in a couple of weeks.

Kira had finished the last bite of alfredo and now we were headed back to the nursing home parking lot. I wanted the night to last forever but I didn't want to keep her out too long. Well, at least not on the first date. By the way she talks and the way things have been going, I'm sure we will see more of each other in the future.

"Well, honey, I had a wonderful evening. I really don't want to keep you out late. I'm sure you have a busy day tomorrow. I do want to say that I look forward to you moving back to town and I am hoping to see you more often. My cousin is getting married in a couple of weeks. I would love nothing more than for you to be my date for the wedding. Would you be interested in going?

"I would love to. I think I can find something to throw on for the event. I love a good wedding, and a fun-filled reception!" Even I myself found the humor in that. By the sound of that comment, she doesn't dress up often. I don't care what she wears, just for her to show up and be my date would satisfy me more than anything right now.

"Great! Not this Saturday but the next. Should I pick you up at your parents' house?"

"That won't be necessary, I'm sure I can find the church and meet you there." Odd that she wouldn't let me come pick her up, but I would also say that it is too soon to give me an opportunity to meet her parents. Right now, all that matters is that she accepted my invitation. I don't think she has anything to hide. If she did, I don't think she would go out anywhere in public and risk her secret being exposed to me. That to me is a sign that she isn't hiding anything. I wrote down the time of the wedding and the address for the church on the back of a spare business card I had in the car. "I guess this is good night. Have a safe trip home and I will see you soon, Kyle. I had a wonderful time as well, bye." She leaned over and hugged me before she opened the door to get out of the car. I watched her get in her car and safely drive off. I sat in the parking lot for a few minutes after she left. I could do nothing but dream for a moment. I was really taking a liking to Kira. I was missing her presence. The thought of her face brought a smile to mine as I started the car and left the parking lot.

Once I got home, I called Marcus to let him know that they would all meet Kira in a couple of weeks. I told him that she would be attending the wedding as my date. I could hear the excitement from Jacs while she was ear hustling in our conversation in the background. I was excited as well. After I got off the phone, I fixed myself a quick drink, laid down for the night. I laid there for the longest staring at the ceiling fan going round and around. All I could think about was the evening we had together, and wonder what the future had in store. For once in my life, I could say that everything was moving at a nice pace. Everything at this moment seemed perfect.

I think Kira is great, and I would love to introduce her to the crew. Hopefully she will fit in and join us at the Hole in the Wall in the future on game nights. I think I will bring her up tomorrow when I talk to Mom.

CHAPTER THREE

The next morning when I woke up, I felt eager to get along with my day. I had a good night last night. Once again, things were going good in my life. I know you shouldn't always base your life on your current situations or circumstances, but with the way things were going, I just felt normal. Today, I didn't mind waking up and getting ready for work. My shower was refreshing, breakfast was delicious, and no matter what I picked to wear today, seemed like the best outfit I owned. The ride to work was even peaceful. Even the song selections that came across the radio seemed to have brought old memories and a smile to my face. When I arrived at work, as I walked through the doors, Mr. Robinson the nursing home's maintenance technician asked me about my date last night? He had mentioned how he saw the lady that came in the nursing home yesterday getting into my car in the parking lot. He gave me a little advice, wished me luck, and sent me on my way. Mr. Robinson was also one of the senior employees here at the nursing home. He lived in a nice house next door to the nursing home. It's funny how people grow and time flies. He must have been in his early to mid-thirties when I would come to volunteer in the afternoons after school. He was always sharing words of wisdom and giving me advice. I remember the times would Mr. Robinson and I would hangout. We would listen to old classical records, play chess in his office, or go to his house and watch sports until mom got off work. I admired Mr. Robinson a lot. Other than my father, he was one of the most important male figures in my life. He told me how he played basketball and football for Highland High. He would have become a professional basketball player, but he couldn't fully recover from a knee injury he had suffered his junior year in college._He had come home and started out working as a janitor for the nursing home. A little after I was born, he went back to school to become a maintenance man here at the facility. He took care of all the electrical work and the responsibilities of the upkeep of the facility. Anything that needed to be fixed or contracted went through Mr. Robinson.

After getting my paperwork together and making my rounds, I stopped by my mother's room. She was located in the far, east wing of the nursing home. The east wing was considered assistant living. It is comprised of residents that require low to no maintenance. My mother didn't really need much looking after at all, it was just that she had gotten older, and didn't want the worries of living alone after my father died. Due to her years of service, the nursing home didn't charge as much monthly for her residency. She was happy here. Even most of her friends were in close living quarters and a few of her co-workers were residents as well. The earlier part of the day was always the best time for me to visit, because a little after noon is when she and the girls would be busy doing their daily routine of cards, working in the garden, TV shows, group conversations about the old days, and sometimes I would catch her and Mr. Robinson playing chess. I deeply loved my mother. She and I have always been close. To have her close to me every day while I worked was an absolute a blessing.

I had brought her breakfast. Being that I had already eaten, I drank coffee while she ate. Marcus and Jacs wedding was the main topic of conversation as we sat and chitchat. She was as excited as I was. Being that both Marcus's parents had passed on, she was going to be sitting in her sister-in-law's place as his mother. She spoke about how close she and her sister-in-law were and how honored she was when Marcus asked her to sit in her place in the wedding. She went on and on about how beautiful her and my father's wedding was and how she hopes to see me married some day before she goes on to be with the Lord. I hadn't told her about Kira, but as we talked about weddings, Kira was in the back of my mind. Suddenly there was a knock at the door and my mother answered from the couch. It was almost time for the girls to stop by. I watched as the door opened.

"I hope I'm not intruding. Mrs. Sharon at the front desk told me where I could find you. She said you were with a resident and it would be okay to go on back." It was Kira with a white box from Alice's with two drinks on top it. I hope I didn't bring about any bad feelings, but I know she noticed the shocking look on my face as she stood in the door way. She started to the couch; I rose to my feet, as my mother welcomed, and escorted her in. Before I could get a word out, she extended her hand to my mother. "Hello, ma'am, how are you today? My name is Kira, I'm a friend of Kyle's."

Though I wanted my mother to meet Kira, I was extremely nervous at this moment. Calmly my mother replied, "Hello, dear, I'm Mrs. McCormic. I'm Kyle's mother." Too shocked to speak, I could only observe the meeting between Kira and my mother. After my mother extended her hand and introduced herself, Kira's smile turned to a look of confusion and her hand dropped down to her side. My mother began to laugh. She looked over at me, and said, "I had forgotten what all my first impressions were like when I introduced myself as your mother. It would always tickle your father and me to death." She looked back at Kira and in a humorous tone and asked, "Am I too much for you, dear? Does my hair look all right?" Patting her hair as she laughed and somewhat posed in front of Kira. "Is there something on my face?" She started wiping the corners of her mouth as she looked back at me. "Am I overly dressed?" Straightening her clothes as she giggled. Her hair was totally fine. She knew she wasn't overly dressed and nothing was on her face. My mother was and still is a beautiful woman, and still considered one of the most beautiful women in town even at her old age. Not to mention the most relaxed woman in the room at this moment.

"No, ma'am, not at all. I just never thought of Kyle's mother to be," Kira replied with a stutter and pause.

"White, darling, go ahead, it's okay. His father and I are white." She finally stopped laughing, reached for Kira's hand and offered her a seat on the couch beside her. "Here, have a seat, dear. Let me explain it to you." Kira sat down beside my mother and I took the chair across from the couch. It wasn't like that I didn't know my mother was white. I didn't even think it to be an issue, but maybe I should have mentioned it to Kira somewhere during the last few conversations we had. I guess I was so concerned with her issues that I had forgotten to mention my own. I had grown to be so comfortable with it that I no longer noticed the color difference. I had dated white girls before. I will admit that there were a few families that didn't accept such a union, but no one had ever really given me grief about interracial relations. The town was predominately white populated. As far as I could remember the town loved both my mother and father, and I don't recall ever being treated unfairly. My mother had told me this story twice in my whole life. Somehow in the midst of this odd situation I needed to hear it again.

"One morning while I was working here at the nursing home, a kitchen aid had found an abandon black newborn baby boy outside the back door of the kitchen. He was in an open suitcase, padded with dry bloody towels, wrapped in a blanket. They had brought him in and cleaned him up. A quite a bit of the staff had already taken a liking to the baby. It was hard to feed him, but somehow I was the first to get him to nurse off a bottle. We had contacted the authorities. Social Services were contacted as well. Instead of them taking him that day, the nurses and I fixed a room for him here at the nursing home. He was cared for around the clock on our lunch breaks. Some nights I would stay here in this room on a spare roll out bed to watch over him. The authorities put out a search for his parents. No one was found, and they were scheduled to come take him during the middle of the following week. A couple days before they were to come take him, my husband and I were talking, and I had broken into tears when I told him that they were coming to take the baby. I guess ones love can be so much for the other; that Kenneth had showed up at the nursing home the day they had come for the baby. He presented me with papers issued by the courts. The courts had granted us temporary custody of the baby until we had the adoption paperwork drawn up. The first time he held him, the baby had easily taken to Kenneth's voice. Kenneth rocked him for about an hour telling him about his younger brother, who he had loved dearly when they were children. Kenneth had lost his brother in a drowning accident in an old water hole they used to swim in behind the local dry cleaners. At the end of the story, the child was given the name Kyle Lucas McCormic. That was the name of Kenneth's brother who had drowned."

My mother had finished her story. The whole time she told the story, I had sat there sipping on the strawberry milkshake Kira had brought, observing the two, and listening as though I was a fly on the wall. For the first time since she had sat down, Kira had finally taken her eyes off my mother and looked across at me. Eyes full of tears she just merely smiled at me. After wiping the tears from her eyes she leaned over and hugged my mother. She told her how much she admired my mother and father for taking me in as abandoned child. "That's a beautiful story, Mrs. McCormic. Was it ever hard to raise him? Did others ever treat you different? Were you and your husband ever treated like lepers or outcast?"

"The first few years were hard. Technically the only friends we had for a long time were the employees at the nursing home and Kenneth's co-workers from the construction company. Kyle's first three or four years of school were difficult for him. At the time of his childhood, I could only remember there being approximately four or five black couples in this town—Mr. Robinson's parents, Mrs. Sharon's family, the Thomas family that owns the downtown drugstore, and the other two couples didn't have any children. Kyle's father and I had spent many nights giving comfort and explaining to him that he was no different than any child at that school. Most people don't respond too well to difference and change. Kyle only had three real friends his whole life, his cousin Marcus, and two others that he had been classmates with his whole life. I'm sure you will love them once you meet them. Kyle even excelled in sports and academics better than most children. We didn't have any trouble out of him growing up. As time had passed, the town had grown to love Kyle. The McComic family name stood alone for itself, but Kyle somehow made a better name for our family. Kenneth and I had tried for years to have children, but it wasn't possible for some reason. He and I both believed that it was God's way of giving us what our hearts had desired for so long. Well, dear, I'm sure you have had enough of me babbling for one day. Kyle would you like to take Miss…?"

"Alexander, my name is Kira Alexander, ma'am."

"Well, Ms. Alexander, it was nice to meet you. Kyle, would you like to take Ms. Alexander for a walk, so you two can talk?"

I went over to my mother, gave her a hug and a kiss goodbye. "I love you and I will see you tomorrow." As I was escorting Kira out the door, I looked back at my mother to tell her, "Don't forget that we have the wedding rehearsal dinner tomorrow. I will be to pick you up around four o'clock."

"It's a date, dear, and I will be sure to look my best!" she replied with a smile as she waived.

I led Kira outside the nursing home. We took a stroll through the courtyard. I'm sure she had some questions about what had just happened. I was nervous thinking that she may never want to see me or even talk to me again.

"Weird day, huh?" I asked her as we were walking.

"Somewhat of a surprise, but I'm not that easy to shock with any past story. I have heard and seen a lot in my past while growing up in an all-girls private school. Your mother seems like an extraordinary lady. I think it is wonderful what she and your father did. From what I have seen so far, you turned out to be an extremely nice gentleman. It is sad how your life started, but you were still blessed to be raised by two loving parents. I don't think it was right for whoever abandoned you, but maybe they felt that they couldn't give you the love and care that was needed. By giving you up, they admitted that they couldn't care for and nurture you like you deserved. I just don't see how anyone could give up their child without at least watching from a distance to make sure they are in good hands and turned out okay. I just know that if I were a mother who abandoned her child, I wouldn't be able to live with myself without knowing or keeping a close undetected watch over that child."

"My mother and father had always believed me to be a blessing. They believed that God saw it fit for me to be conceived by whoever my parents were, but somehow for me to end up in their care. I myself even believe in God and that he works in ways that we do not understand but he always has our best interest at heart. I have no memory of my biological parents, so missing them wasn't a problem. Do you and your parents often tell your niece stories of her parents?"

"Yes, quite often, especially when she comes to stay with me. I talk about her mother to her a lot. I kind of want her to feel like she knew or knows her real mother. I always tell her funny stories about her mother, her likes and dislikes, and how she and her mother are similar in so many ways. Chelsie and I have a close relationship. I care for her like she is my own daughter. I am so proud of her."

Although Kira did not meet my mother like I expected or would have liked her to, the experience gave us a chance to get to know one another more on a personal level. I was glad she didn't run out of the nursing home in shock. After a long walk around the nursing home, we ended up at Kira's car.

"Well, I must admit today was some kind of experience. I'm glad you came to see me today."

She looked me in the eyes and said, "I figured I would surprise you with some cheesecake from our favorite cafe. I guess you could say that I was the one that was a little more surprised out of the equation. It was good to meet your mother. I think she is a beautiful lady. She and her husband raised a handsome man. I will see you later, Kyle. Call me." She smiled, hugged, and kissed me on the cheek as she turned to get in her car to leave.

After it was time to get off work, I called Jacs and asked her if she wanted to grab a bite to eat. I wasn't really all that hungry; I just needed someone to talk to. I could always rely on her to give me an honest opinion or answer whether it hurt my feelings or not. She agreed to meet me at the Chinese restaurant on the other side of town.

"So, cousin, what's on your mind now?" she asked, laughing after the waiter folded up our menus and left.

I started to pretend as though I didn't know what she was talking about, but she and I have always had a close relationship growing up. It has always been hard to hide much from her. "It's Kira. What do you think about interracial relations? I mean, you, the fellas, and me have been friends since the sandbox. I am the only black sheep out of the flock. How do you feel about me? All these years coming up and nothing was said. No indifferences between us. Did you for once ever see my complexion and wonder?"

"No, kids don't see color, Kyle. We were innocent when we all met. Strange that your parents were white at the time but we all loved you no matter what color you were. I'm sure the guys asked their parents when we were children. If they were anything like mine when I asked, then we loved and cared for you despite what you looked like or how you got here. I know the world isn't color blind and at times mixing and mingling has its boundaries to others. To me, it's about two individuals who engage in the laws of attraction. Most families didn't accept it when we were younger but once they had gotten to know you, it faded. People in this town love you Kyle McCormic. We love you. Although I must ask, what brings about this concern of your color? Twenty-five-plus years of friendship and thousands of conversations under the influence of alcohol, not once have you ever asked such a question."

"Kira met Mother today," I replied while staring off into the restaurant. "For the first time in my life, I had felt like an outcast. As my mother explained to Kira why she and my father were white, I felt different. Somehow inside, I felt abandonment and pity. I thought to myself, here I had been doing my research on the Alexanders and Kira like some unsolved mystery when my life is the biggest unsolved mystery in this town. No one knows who my parents are or were. What right did I have to have any suspicion about Kira?"

"Well, one thing is obvious. You really like this girl. I don't think she has a problem with you being black or you wouldn't have gotten this far. Relax, Kyle." She reached across the table, grabbed my hands and said, "I am happy for you and I can't wait to meet her. I really hope she is the one for my best friend. I grow tired of running off all the unworthy women and high-class whores you and Trent bring home."

Jacs was right. I shouldn't have anything to worry about. I guess today just caught me off guard. I never really wondered who my real parents were. Part of what Kira said made me wonder why they did abandon me and not try to make sure I was okay. I truly wonder what would possess a person or two people to leave a child abandoned on a doorstep. Jacs and I had a few more laughs, a couple more drinks, then I found myself back home. Once I got home with today still lingering on my mind, I poured myself another drink, put on some music, then pulled out some old photo albums. They were of the crew and me when we were in high school. There was hardly ever a dull moment with us. I was truly blessed to have such friends in my life. I had also, run across some old nursing home photos Mother had taken when she had worked there. As I turned the pages, I started to notice more and more how much I stuck out in all the photos. I was the only black person in every photo except for the school picture. Every photo was full of smiles and laughter. Not once did I think about my color as I stood in the midst of everybody posing for a picture. My color never stopped me from having a good time with friends and family. I don't know why such a thing bothers me now, when it didn't all those years. I began to think, what did people think of me in school and in college? How did the town start to view me? I was involved in everything positive that I could get into. I wasn't antisocial. I was always in the in crowd. Was it truly friendship or were people just being nice because they didn't want to make an impression on themselves? Could it be because of who my parents were? How did black people think of me? I even began to think about all my dating experiences. I don't discriminate against black women, but I noticed that there was a tendency in dating more outside of my race than inside my race. I mean, there wasn't much of an option here in town, but college was well diverse. I began to wonder if people really loved and accepted me for me. Now it seems like my life was some sad movie with everyone watching, crying near the end, and feeling sorry for the poor black boy who had gotten abandoned as a newborn. All night I sat there flipping through albums, thinking and drinking. I drank myself to sleep right there in the recliner near the fireplace.

CHAPTER FOUR

I had woken the next morning in the recliner, still in my attire from yesterday. I got up to shower and get ready for work. By the looks of the time, I'm going to be late, no need to rush. I got myself dressed and headed out the door. I wasn't in the best of moods and I could tell today was going to be a long day. I felt like doing nothing. Today is the day we have Jacs and Marcus dinner. At this moment, I don't even feel like going. Heck, I didn't feel like going to work neither. I rarely miss work. I like my career, but it's mainly because I get to see my mother every day. Mother, she's not even my real mother. Forgive me, Lord; that was disrespectful. For the first time in my life, I truly felt different. I felt like I didn't belong. Every time I saw my reflection, I noticed my complexion. I'm the best man in my cousins wedding. Cousin, we aren't really related. Heck, we don't even have the slightest resemblance and we are first cousins. Suddenly, my family is not my family. I am going to look like a fool. I am the best man at my first cousins wedding. The only black man in the wedding, if not the building.

Once I pulled up in the parking lot of the nursing home, I sat in my car for a minute. No one knew what I was thinking or going through. At this moment, I didn't even want to face the public or my co-workers. I took a couple takes in my review mirror, trying to remove the look of disgust off my face. I finally got out of the car and entered the nursing home. I hope nobody notices. If I can put on a facade for the day, maybe I will make it all right. As I entered, I stopped by to pick up my folder at the front desk. Mrs. Sharon always had my paperwork organized and ready for me every morning.

"Good morning, Kyle. Long night last night?" Looking over me as though something looked out of place. To be honest, I felt out of place.

"Yes, ma'am. Last night was pretty rough. Just got a lot on my mind, I reckon."

"I know how that can be at times," she replied. "I'm sure whatever it is that is bothering you isn't worth your worry. Don't get worked up over life and its circumstances. Give me a shout if you need to talk."

"Will do, Mrs. Sharon, thank you." *I'm sure she could help*, I thought to myself sarcastically. She goes home to someone of the same color. She belongs to and visits her black family members for the holidays. It's one thing to not really be related to your family, but to not even be of the same race? I look nothing like my family. There isn't one person I know that I can actually say that I am related to. More and more, I am starting to feel like I am on another planet or a foreigner in a strange land.

I stopped by the break room, fixed myself a cup of coffee, and headed to my office. My inner thoughts were overwhelming me. I could feel me removing myself, although nobody was around. For a couple of hours, I had buried myself in paperwork. I was doing my best not to leave my office. Afternoon was approaching and I was thinking of a thousand excuses not to go visit my mother. If Mrs. Sharon could spot something wrong with me, then I know my own mother would. Well, not really my mother, just the woman who took me in because she felt pity on the poor abandoned black child in the suitcase. I really don't like looking at it that way, but how else should I look at it? Suddenly, everything around me felt fictitious. I don't even feel like I am who I really am. Like a white man trapped in a black body. Better yet, a black man trapped in a white body, but no one notices I'm really black.

There was a knock at my door. There was Mr. Robinson standing in my doorway. "Hey, son, your mother and I were just talking about you. I had stopped by to visit her today. Your name had come up and she started to wonder where you were as she looked at her clock. She said you normally come by at this time of the day. She thought you may not be here or something was wrong. As I left, I told her I would stop by and check on you. Is everything all right?"

I responded immediately with, "Long night last night, sir! Had a few things on my mind and lost track of time. I reckon I'd better get down there and see my mother." I truly want to know what he thought after I referred to a white lady as my mother. Ironic how the first two people I meet today at work are black. I closed my folder and headed out of my office.

Mr. Robinson stopped me as I was walking out of my office. "Son, my door is always open if you need to talk. Even if you don't want to talk about it, our old chess board awaits us." He smiled, patted me on the shoulder, and walked away. Mr. Robinson and I spent quite a lot of our spare time at work throughout the weeks playing chess and chitchatting. Every now and then, we attend a game or two here and there at the high schools. Mr. Robinson is the only black person I do interact with, always have my whole life. Other than my mother, he and I will more than likely have a conversation in the future about what I am feeling today. My being late or not stopping by is enough to strike my mother's interest. I really don't want to talk about it but I don't want to not see my mother today neither. More and more I am feeling confused on whether or not to even call her my mother anymore.

I knocked on the door as I entered her quarters. "Hello, dear! I was worried something might be wrong. You are usually here by now." She was straightening up her kitchen area as I came in. She hadn't even looked at me. "Is everything all right?"

"Good as always I reckon." I tried to maintain tone and posture as though nothing was the matter. I sat down on the couch. She followed me into the living room and sat down beside me.

"What's the matter, dear? I can already tell you are not yourself." She put her hand on my knee and scooted closer beside me.

Avoiding eye contact, I focused on the hand that was on my knee. "What makes you think something is wrong, Mother?"

"Well, every day you come to visit me, you find me no matter where I am in this place. Normally I get a hug and a kiss before you make yourself at home. Plus, it's not like you to be late. Above all, you're my son. Mothers have a sense of knowing these things when it comes to their children."

Without hesitating, I responded, "How could you have that sense with me? I'm not really your son. You didn't birth me. How do you figure that you and I have that same connection? Forgive me, Mother, but we have no genetic ties. Mother, Brenda, Mrs. McCormic, or whatever I should call you. I don't even know what to call you at this moment? How could you figure we have that bond?" At this moment, my insides were crumbling into a thousand pieces. I didn't want or mean to hurt her but I must know. With a response like that, she had every right to smack the taste out of my mouth and send me on my way. Instead, she had a calm look on her face, but I could see the tears accumulating in her eyes. Even though she tried to remain calm, I could tell those words had torn her heart from her chest. I felt like a monster for what I was saying, but what was the right thing to say? At this time, I couldn't process the right words to say to bring the situation to light in more calm tone.

"Did someone say something to you, Kyle? Was it that girl? What would bring about such questions and attitude? What could have happened to fill your mouth with such words?" She wiped her tears and took a deep sigh. "You're right. I never experienced the joy of birthing whom I count as my only son. One thing I can testify to is that I am your mother. I have loved you more than the one that had given birth to you and more than anyone else could. I don't love you out of pity or for charity. Does your complexion take away my right of being your mother? Your complexion has never stopped me from trying to give you the best or wanting what is best for you. If that were the case, then I don't think God would have allowed it thirty six years ago. Love has no limits, and it certainly knows no color. No matter how you look at me. If you want to call me mother or not, I will always love you. I am sure all this is tough for you at this time. I imagine you have never had time to really think about it until now. I wish I had all the answers, but the only answer is to continue to love you no matter what course you take in the matter. My love for you overrides everything that causes those contradicting thoughts lingering in your mind."

"I'm sorry, Mother. I know we have never had this discussion before. I have never even thought of having it before today. Kira has said nothing to me about it, but this does have to do with what happened yesterday. You will always be my mother. I do love you more than anything in this world. It's just that now I have this feeling of loneliness. I have no blood ties with anyone in this town. Not a long lost sister or distant cousin. The only people of color that are closed to me are Mr. Robinson and Mrs. Sharon. I have known them since you have been bringing me here. There is no one left other than them. Out of all the people in this world, how did I get to be the abandoned child? What woman or man would do such a thing? With the way today's society is, I could understand being raised by a mother with no father or maybe vice versa, but neither? Did no one come looking for me? Was there any rumor of a black couple having a child? It's as though I fell out of the sky."

"I'm sorry, dear. If I could ease the pain then I would do whatever it would take, but that's something we all have to accept. All I know is that God did not create you without purpose. Not to be left alone in this world, and certainly not to fall by the wayside. You have been such a blessing to me and your father. I remember you would always ask Kenneth and me for a baby brother. You were too young to understand, but I couldn't have children. Kenneth and I had tried for years. We prayed and asked God to bless us with a child for many years." She started to smile and laugh as she wiped the tears away from her face. "God speaks to us in ways that seem unusual to us at times. I felt it deep in my heart when I first saw the abandoned child. I could hear the question running through my mind as clear as a natural voice in the room. 'How can you pray for so many years and abandon this child who needs what you have promised me to give?' Kenneth said he heard the same question. No matter how you look at it, how you feel, or what you may say, you will always be the son of Kenneth and Brenda McCormic."

I felt a little at ease after my mother's testimony and tears. I adored my mother, and I would never intentionally do anything to hurt her. The words of her story and the emotion on her face overwhelmed my heart. I have never known my real mother and may never meet her. I don't truly know what the love bond between a real mother and son may feel like, but my feelings for her can be compared to or greater than any other sons to his mother. I can't say the pain is completely gone, but I do have to find a way to pull myself together before the wedding dinner tonight. I don't want any more attention than I have now about how I am feeling. Plus, I don't want to ruin Jacs and Marcus's big moment.

"Well, I must get back to work, Mother. Thank you for the talk. I love you. I am thankful for what you and Father have done for me. It takes courage and love to do what you two and the rest of the family have done for me. To me, you will always be the most wonderful woman in the world." I wrapped my arm around her and pulled her close to me. I squeezed her tightly and kissed her on her forehead. As I was heading out the door, I looked back and said, "Don't forget that we have a date tonight and I will be to pick you up in couple of hours."

Heading back to my office, I ran into Mr. Robinson. "Did everything go okay with you and your mother? I was on my way to check on you, guys. You sure you don't want to talk about it over a game of chess? The board and pieces are starting to collect a little dust. I thought about how long it's been while I was cleaning it off yesterday. So what do you say?" he asked as he smiled and gave me a soft slug on the shoulder.

"No, sir, not today. I'm sure we will discuss it in the future." As I walked off, I thought to myself, *Good ole Mr. Robinson, always there for me. In life we all have that one person who isn't a relative that has been there since we could remember, lending a helping hand. That person was Mr. John David Robinson.*

As I arrived back to my office and sat down, it had struck me that I haven't talked to Kira today. I don't think I should bother her right now. Plus, I'm sure that she is probably spending a little quality time with her niece. In a way, Kira is a little bit similar to my mother, trying to help her parents raise her sister's child. I can only sympathize for the little girl after feeling what I have been feeling for the last day and a half.

I finished what little bit of work that I had left. After my work was done, I went to my mother's room, picked her up, and took her home with me so I could get ready. Nothing was said on the way home. The whole ride home, she stared out the window at the scenery as we passed by. She held my hand the all the way to the house. When she decided to take up her residence in the nursing home, she left me with the house, so she was well acquainted with the house when she came to visit. I didn't really change anything but the furniture. She would always go in father's old study and dig out old photos, placing them in blank photo albums in the closet. I never really sat down to look at the albums in his study that she would put together. I mainly just looked at the ones that she and I would create together. It was her way of spending quality time with me. I really wasn't all that interested in doing such organizing, but I knew she loved it, and that is why I would participate. Every time she would come home with me, she would light a fire in the fireplace and organize the old photos.

When it was time to go to the dinner, she had gathered up two shoe boxes full of photos and an album, "Place these in the trunk for me, dear. I want to organize an album back at my place at the residence." I had asked no questions. She was always doing things like that with photos. She used to tell me how she enjoyed the memories as she went through each photo. Sometimes she would say that she was visiting her memory bank. Dad used to joke and say that she was trying to stay sharp in the head and fight off Alzheimer's. I escorted her to the passenger side of the car. I had placed the album and the photos on the floor board of the vehicle behind her. Once I got in the car, she placed her hand on my thigh and asked, "Are you okay?"

"Yes, Mother, I will be okay." Sighing as I responded to the question. It didn't matter if I was or I wasn't feeling well, I had to pull it together before we made it to the dinner. I had been waiting for this day since the two announced their engagement. With the way I am feeling at this moment, I could use another month or two down the road. As we arrived at the church for the wedding rehearsal, Aunt Tina and Uncle Kevin were standing outside to escort us in. The two greeted us as we stepped out of the vehicle. Aunt Tina wasn't Marcus's real mother. Aunt Lisa was lost in a car crash. She was on her way to one of Marcus's football games while he was in college, when her car hydroplaned into oncoming traffic. Aunt Tina was good to Marcus. It seemed as though she came in and picked up right where Aunt Lisa left off. The family took to her quickly. I think she may have reminded Uncle Kevin of the kind of woman Aunt Lisa was.

I was received by Uncle Kevin with a hug as I stepped out of the car. "How's my favorite nephew?" Laughing as he gave me one of his famous bear hugs he had always greeted the boys with as we were growing up. *Yeah, your favorite black sheep of the family*, I had thought to myself as he hugged me. Uncle Kevin was the oldest out of my dad and Uncle Kyle. They were fairly big men. Mom said that they were both athletes and farm hands coming up. She would always tell me that Uncle Kevin was the toughest out of the bunch. He and dad ran the family business once they turned of age. He took 100 percent ownership of the business after dad died of cancer, but he has always given dad's share to my mother and I ever since. He made sure that she and I never wanted for anything. We were well taken care of. Mother never sought to find another husband after dad died. She said that he was her Prince Charming and no other man ever walked the earth greater than he. I really felt bad for what I was thinking. As good as he has been to Mother and me, it was disrespectful to even think such a thought. We proceeded to escort Aunt Tina and mother into the church for rehearsal.

"Kevin, this is beautiful!" Mother sounded breathless as she was at awe at the sight of how beautifully the church had been decorated. The walls had been draped with shiny yellow silk banners, showcasing the married couple's initials on them. Yellow, white, and red roses had been placed at the end of every row as you walked down the aisle. The altar had an arch of yellow, red, and white roses. It had a large candle underneath it to be lit by the couple during the ceremony. It was truly beautiful.

We were greeted by Jacs, Marcus, and the wedding coordinator at the front of the aisle. Jacs did not want a big flashy spectacle. I was Marcus's best man, and Trent was a groomsman. Jacs had her sister as her maid of honor and her best friend from work as her bridesmaid.

Everybody loves a wedding, and not to mention a reception. Marcus and Jacs were pretty well loved in this town. I imagine the church will be full of people, with the addition of everybody and their mama at the reception. I started to wonder what things are going to be like with Kira here at the wedding and at the reception. God, I hope she shows up.

After the wedding rehearsal, we went over to the church cafeteria to eat. Jacs, Marcus, and the wedding party sat across the room from Mother and me. I was keeping a distance, using my mother as an excuse. I really wasn't in the mood, and I didn't want to spoil all the fun and laughs. As I was eating, I could feel my mother place her hand on my thigh under the table. "Is everything all right? I know I have asked already, but you have been quiet the whole time. You shouldn't be so distant from your friends over there. Acting concerned for me is no excuse. I am well all right," she mumbled as we never made eye contact, gazing over at the commotion. "Now you do your mother a favor. Put this issue up for now. Put a smile on your face, go over there, and enjoy this moment with your friends. It's a special time in their life. Neither them, nor I want to remember Kyle distancing himself the whole time."

I finished my dinner, emptied my plate, grabbed a glass of water, and joined the group. After sitting and hearing the first few laughs about all the silly incidents that went on back in the day, it didn't take long for me to forget what was bothering me and join in the stroll down memory lane. We had a lot of fun coming up together, good times, and bad times. I'm glad Mother pulled me out of my pit of pity and made me stop being anti-social. I realized that I was being selfish and could have possibly ruined a good memory about this special time in Jacs and Marcus's life.

It was getting late; Jacs had already left for home and bed. The fellas had thought it would be a good idea to head to the Hole in the Wall for a few drinks. Uncle Kevin volunteered to take mother back the nursing home so I could leave with the gang. Before she left, she reminded me of the photos in the car. I gave Uncle Kevin the keys and told him to leave them behind the rear driver side tire for me when I get back. I kissed my mother goodbye and left with the Marcus and Trent.

"So did you invite Cinderella to your favorite cousins wedding?" Marcus asked as we were being seated at our table.

"Yes, I did. She accepted the invitation. Now, I just hope she shows up. I don't want to spend the day looking at the door wondering if she will show or not."

"Why do you doubt that she will show? Haven't you guys been out a few times? Plus, didn't she come visit you at work a couple times? What have you got to worry about? Sounds like to me, that this one is in the bag little cousin," Marcus replied.

"Yeah, she did visit me at the nursing home. That's the problem. She met mother on one of her visits," I, in turn, answered with my eyes on the table.

"She met Aunt Brenda? Well, that's a good thing. My Aunt Brenda is great gal. If anything, I know she added some cool points to your side of the scoreboard. Everybody loves Aunt Brenda." Laughing as he seemed filled with excitement due to the fact the Kira met my mother.

A serious look came over my face as I then looked Marcus and Trent in the eyes. "You two don't see me? Do you not see who or what I am? How would you feel meeting me and then meeting my mother, my white mother at that? How many black men do you know that were raised by white families? As a matter of fact, how many of my family members have you met?" I then grabbed my coat and started for the door. No sooner than I could get out the door, Trent and Marcus followed.

Trent asked as he put his arm around my shoulder. "Is there something you need to talk about?"

I took a deep sigh and stared off into the moon out across the parking lot. "Has my color ever bothered either one of you? I need you two to be honest with me right now. Has the fact that I'm probably the only black friend you have ever had been a concern to either of you? It's important to me to know guys. The harsh reality of my past has hit me for the first time in my life. I feel alone. Lately I have been questioning who I am, and are the people in my life real?"

Marcus stepped ahead of us; hands shoved down in his coat pockets, gazing across the parking lot, and beginning to say, "I've asked my father about it a time or two. I admit that I have had concerns. I still have the same concerns today. I wonder everyday how could any human being ever abandon such person as you, Kyle? I look at you some days and wonder how could my best friend, my closest family member, be of no blood relation, and black? I have never been closer to anyone in or outside of my family than I have been to you. I wonder how the world could be so divided by race and color at times, when the man I feel closer to than a brother isn't related to me and black?" He then turned to me and looked me in the eyes, "You're like a brother to me, Kyle. Black, white, blue, green, yellow, blood, or no blood. I have considered you no less than my brother. If you ask me, God never intended for anything negative to happen to any of us. Even though you ended up abandoned by your real parents. God sure placed you in the care of people that would love you just as much or even more. This is a family, friendship, and bond that God used to display to a piece of the world how truly deep His love is! I think I speak for all of us when I say that I wouldn't have it, or you, any other way."

Trent pulled a little tighter. "All things being fair and equal, I agree with Marcus. I honestly don't know a better guy than you. I used to wonder the same thing as a child. We all were created by God. Whatever circumstance we end up in may not be of his choosing but he has always taken our negative and turned it into our positive."

The three of us came together for a hug. "You will always be family to us, cousin. We mean that, and don't you ever forget it. Don't let no one or nothing cause you to think different," Marcus said as we all were huddled together.

We all jumped in Trent's car and headed back to the church. Once I had gotten home, I lit the fireplace, threw on an old record, and poured myself a drink. As I drank and watched the flames flicker, I hoped for a wonderful day tomorrow. How it would be nice to have Kira there. I was truly missing her smile and the warmth of her presence. I could tell that I was really falling for her. She seemed so perfect in every way to me. I smiled as I began to picture her and

43

myself dancing at the reception. I wonder if she could dance at all. I hadn't heard from her all day. I sure hope she doesn't stand me up tomorrow.

CHAPTER FIVE

The next day I had decided I would sleep in a little bit. I didn't have to work that day. The wedding wasn't until the mid-part of the afternoon. Catching up on some sleep did not sound like a bad idea. It all had seemed like a good plan, but the smell of breakfast downstairs had drawn me out of my slumber. It smelled delicious. Being that I am the only one living here, who could be in my house fixing breakfast? As I made way down the stairs, I could hear the sound of dishes and laughs. As I entered the kitchen, I saw Mr. Robinson drinking coffee at the island and my mother at the stove cooking. Who, what, and how of my curiosity had been answered, but why still remained?

Mr. Robinson turned to me with a smile and laughter in his voice, "Hey, son! Good morning there. Your mother caught me in the dining room of the nursing home this morning. She stopped me as I was getting ready to order my breakfast. She told me that she would like to spend the day with her son before the wedding. After bribing me with breakfast, I was reminded of how good her breakfast, lunch, and dinner was when I used to do yard work and construction for your father during the summer. It didn't take much, but I was convinced that I needed to take the day off and give her ride out to the old house."

"Good morning, dear! Here you go, John. I believe French toast, ham, and eggs used to be your favorite." She then turned to me smiling. "I believe a sausage and cheese omelet has always been your favorite my dear. I added a little spice to it like you like it as well." She then poured Mr. Robinson some more coffee and me a glass of orange juice. After serving us, she fixed her plate and joined us for breakfast.

"What did you and the boys get into last night? Did you sleep well?" My mother asked as she was sitting herself on a stool across from me.

"We didn't do much last night. We went for a few drinks and some more laughs. We had a good talk last night. They are like my brothers. I think the heart to heart we had last night brought some clarity to some the things I had been thinking about. If not at all, it strengthened our bond." Goodness! Mother still hasn't lost her touch in the kitchen. Like Mr. Robinson, I had forgotten how good her cooking was, but I was well reminded this morning. "After the boys and I left, I came home, poured myself a drink, lit the ole fire place, and relaxed in the study." I then turned to Mr. Robinson. "You know that old record we would listen to at your house, the one we also listen to while playing chess in your office? I had bought it at an old record store while I was off in college. A lot of days I come home, pour myself a drink, light the fire in the study, throw on that record, sit back, and unwind."

"Oh yeah, I sure love that record? What is it that you have been thinking about? Is something bothering you?" he asked.

"Not now, sir, maybe over a game of chess in the future. Today seems to be starting off pretty good, let's not ruin it with something that isn't so important." We continued to enjoy our breakfast. Mr. Robinson and I started reminiscing about the old days. As Mother sat there observing the laughter and us strolling down memory lane. As we went on and on, I realized how he had taught me a lot and had always been there for me. He taught me how to ride a bike, play sports, chess, dominos, and fish. He even would give me all sorts of financial advice after he finished school. I remember one time my parents were out of town, and asked Mr. Robinson to housesit. Trent and Marcus ended up spending the whole week while my parents were gone. It was more like four roommates than a man babysitting three young teenage boys. He attended most of my sporting events throughout the time of me being involved in athletics. He was also in attendance at my high school and college graduation. He even washed, filled my car with gas, and even bought my tux for my high school prom.

I have always been fond of Mr. Robinson and he was always fond of our family. He and Mother started telling me about how they had taken care of him when he was a child. No he didn't live with them, but he spent a lot of time around my mother and father. He said that his mother had a gambling problem. She had left him to his father when he was about nine years old. His father was an abusive alcoholic and didn't have much to do with him unless it involved verbal abuse or violence. At one time, his father had forbidden him to even set foot on my parent's property. So my father devised a plan that his father would immediately take interest to. My father told his father that he would give Mr. Robinson work and pay him a wage. His father thought it would be a great idea. That way he could save his money then take what little money Mr. Robinson had made and spend it on alcohol. Well, at least that is what he was led to believe. My father did indeed pay Mr. Robinson, but he would only give him a small portion of the earnings to bring home and be taken by his father for alcohol. My parents had opened a savings account and college fund for Mr. Robinson. Although he worked for my parents, he was able to go to school every day, play basketball, and enjoy a normal life. It was the first time in my life that I had ever heard this story. I guess that is why Mr. Robinson is so fond of me after all. He never really had a family neither. He had never experienced any other bond, other than what he had with my parents. He taught me everything my father had taught him, because like me, his real father was never there. As I thought about that story and looked back on my life, I understood how the town could love my parents. I could never repay them for what they have done for me. I could never do anything to equal what they had done for Mr. Robinson.

We sat there reminiscing and laughing until the morning had passed. After two plates and three cups of coffee, Mr. Robinson had finally left. Mother and I continued to talk as we cleaned up the kitchen. She told me that she understood how I was feeling. She told me how proud she and my father were. As the day went on, Mother and I had cleaned a few rooms and rearranged some furniture. Before we knew it, it was time to start getting dressed for the wedding.

"Wow, I mean, wow! Mother, you look beautiful," I said as she stepped into my bedroom while I was in front of the mirror putting the finishing touches on my tux. My mother was in her mid-sixties. Some would say she hides it well. Her personality, her smile, and her physical beauty give off a ray of sunshine every time I look at her. Her presence always demanded attention. My mother was always overflowing with laughter and happiness. It didn't matter the mood, she changed every atmosphere or environment she was in. To me, God couldn't have made a more beautiful creature.

She reached for my neck tie as she approached. "Here, let me get that for you my dear. I used to do this for your father all the time." She straightened my collar, fixed my flower, and brushed my shoulders off. Once we had finished getting dressed, I escorted her to the car, and we were off to the church.

There were people all over the place, hanging out in the parking lot, and lined up outside of the church. Mother and I entered the church from the side entrance to avoid the crowd. When we entered the church, I flagged down Uncle Kevin and the wedding coordinator. She and Uncle Kevin escorted mother to the area where they would stand before they entered sanctuary. I turned and started racing to the other side of the church. As came around the corner, I was stopped in my tracks. She couldn't see me as her back was turned to me, but there she was. The day had been going so well that I had forgotten she was coming. I was at awe once more. I wasn't so quick to speak. I wanted to gaze upon her beauty for a moment. She looked absolutely astonishing. She had on a shimmering satin emerald green evening gown that cling to her like it was painted to every curve of her physique. Her hair was up, revealing the beauty of her shoulders.

I quietly approached her and said, "Ab-so-lute-ly gorgeous!" She slowly turned around with a smile on her face. Smiling back and sarcastically speaking, I spoke softly. "Excuse me, miss. You seem to be lost. Perhaps I can help? Are you a relative to either member of the wedding party? Surely your date for the wedding wouldn't have let such an amazing beauty too far out of his sight now, would he?"

"Um, no, sir. I'm looking for my date. His name is Kyle McCormic. I think he is the best man to the groom. Would you happen to know him?"

"Yes, I think I might know where he is. Here, take a seat while I go get him for you." I took her by the hand and escorted her to the usher to be seated.

"Hey, cousin, are you trying to give me a heart attack or what?" Marcus asked as he and Trent were short of breath coming around the corner. I reckon it turns out they had been looking for me as well. We hurried to join the pastor in the back of the church at the door entrance to the sanctuary behind the altar.

The church was filled with the town's people. The wedding music began to play as we made our way onto the altar in front of the congregation. It was a sweet ceremony. Jacs looked extraordinary. She set off a glow of radiance as she walked down the aisle. Jacs had been a tomboy since day one, but she always captured every man's attention every time she dressed up. I looked over the crowd until Kira and I had finally made eye contact. Her smile was so beautiful. I began to envision what it would be like to experience a moment like this with Kira. I really like this girl. I am so glad that she accepted me for who I am and what she sees, knowing everything about me now. The wedding went on, then the two exchange their vows along with the rings. The wedding was sealed with the traditional kiss. Now my favorite couple is legally and spiritually united.

As we stood outside the church to shake hands, exchange hugs, and thank all the guests, I grabbed Kira, and signaled for mom and Uncle Kevin. I handed her off to my mother, "Please make sure she makes it to the reception." Mother smiled once she recognized who it was. She took her by the hand and Kira joined them on the limousine ride to the reception. When I turned back to shaking hands with the guest, Trent looked over at me with a smile and winked.

As he and I were in the car on the way to the reception hall he asked, "Was that Cinderella in the green gown?"

"Yes! That is Kira Alexander," I replied.

"That girl is gorgeous? She is way more beautiful than I had imagined. You sure she likes black guys?" he asked with laughter in his voice. "Bro, I'm only kidding. I know you really like her, and by the way she responded to you back at the church, I can tell she digs you also."

"You think so?" I asked.

"Sure! Trust me. I know these kinds of things. In my experience, women that only want to be friends will only take you so far. She, my friend, is in to you!" Like I said before, Trent wasn't much of the lady's man that he would like to think himself to be. So I was praying that he was right with what he was saying about this situation.

You could hear the music playing from outside the reception hall when we arrived. Once we entered, everyone was having a great time, dancing with cup in hand. Now Trent, he immediately began the hunt. With no hesitation he stepped out on to the floor to mingle with all the single ladies at the party. Me, I had to find Kira. I had found her, Mom, Uncle Kevin, Marcus, and Jacs in the kitchen area.

"There is my best man! It's about time you showed up. Your mother was just introducing us to Ms. Kira Alexander." As he spoke, you could tell that Marcus was already full of liquor and laughter.

"Yes, she is truly someone special," I replied, as I was looking Kira in the eyes.

"It was a pleasure to meet all of you. Congratulations to the both of you, Mr. and Mrs. McCormic," Kira chimed in. She seemed to be fitting in well by the way she sounded when she spoke to Jacs and Marcus. "Mrs. McCormic, would you mind if I stole your son away for a dance and some conversation?"

"He is all yours, dear. I'm sure he has been anticipating this moment," Mother replied as she smiled at me.

Kira gave her a hug. Then took me by the hand and led me to the dance floor.

As we walked out onto the dance floor, the party was jumping. Suit coats had been flung into every corner of the room, neck ties were loosened, every hair do on the floor had been sweated out, and high heels were placed on every table around the room. Kira and I didn't share too much conversation during the first four or five songs. By the way she was moving, I could tell that she was having fun and really liked to dance. The music finally slowed down as the night progressed. I felt so uplifted with Kira in my arms. I felt as though I was floating on air. The soothing comfort of her body against mine and the softness of her skin from her arms wrapped around my neck made me feel as though I was at peace in her presence. The mood was set and the atmosphere was filled with love as she and I were cheek to cheek, slow dancing out on the dance floor.

"You have a beautiful family, Kyle. I really like your mother. She is so kind and loving. She loves you very much. She and I had a nice heart to heart in the limousine ride on the way over here. I thought it was sweet how she held my hand the whole way here. I told her how perfect I think you are. She in return told me that she thinks her son has fallen hard for me. Is that true, Kyle, have you fallen for me?" She then drew her face back to look me in the eyes, waiting for my response.

There was nothing that I could say to describe or show Kira how I was starting to feel about her. I just leaned forward and we shared our first kiss that night at the reception. For a moment, it seemed like everybody in the reception hall disappeared and it was only her and me. I started dreaming of the future as she was in my arms. I was feeling as though she was the only woman in the world that I desired to spend my life with. I did not want this night to end. I could see my mother across the dance floor. She was standing there watching us with a smile on her face. I could tell that she could sense how good her son was feeling at this moment.

Although, there was still much to uncover and experience, things were going well. She has met my mother, my closest friends, and been introduced to some personal areas in my life. I have yet to meet her parents, her favorite niece, or experience any part of her lifestyle.

CHAPTER SIX

The experience that I had last night was so wonderful that I had to tell someone about it. So I got up, got dressed, and called Mr. Robinson for a game of chess. It had been a while since we had sat down and talked. Besides, he was the only one that I personally knew that wasn't at the wedding. The whole time I was getting dressed, I kept reminiscing about last night. It was truly a "cloud nine" experience. I did not want to wear off the affect that Kira had left on me last night. I thought about calling her but at the end of the night, I remember her saying that she and Chelsie had plans today. After I had gotten dressed, I started straightening up around the house. It wasn't too long after that I heard a knock at the door, it was Mr. Robinson.

"Hey, son!" He had a big smile on his face with excitement in his voice. I guess he had been waiting for us to have this game since it has been so long. I had not forgotten about my troubled episode a couple days ago neither. I'm sure he hasn't forgotten and will ask about that as well.

"Come on in, sir! I was just straightening up the house a little bit. I had to find something to pass the time while I was anticipating humiliating you on the board today." Mr. Robinson laughed at the gesture as he followed me to the old study.

As we entered the study, Mr. Robinson stopped at the old record player and placed the needle on the record. "Perhaps a little theme music while I make you beg for mercy." He and I were both good at playing chess, but I will admit that he is the better player. If we were to keep score of wins and losses, I'm sure he would be in the lead. "So how was the wedding last night? Did that pretty girl show up?"

"The wedding was nice. I believe everybody in the whole town was there except for you. Pretty girl, why would you assume that I would take a date?" I'm sure he noticed the sneakiness in my voice and smile as I tried to seem curious of how he would know.

"I saw you drop her off that one night I was working late at the nursing home. Then there was the look on your face the next day you came in and not to mention I saw her at the nursing home with you out in the courtyard. Being that I have known you all your life, I haven't seen you so serious about a female like you are with this one. I can tell you have taken a real interest in her. She seems to be interested in you as well. Has she met Mrs. Brenda yet?"

"Yes, she met Mother the day you saw us both in the courtyard together. It was an awkward moment, something I truly was not prepared for." After I said that, I knew it was time to talk about what had been bothering me the other day. Somehow it seems like he knows something. As I thought about the series of questions he had asked, it was no different than us playing chess or any other game. He had set me up to come to him and reveal myself.

"I remember you acting strange after that day. That was the day you seemed off balance. You weren't much for looking me in the eyes or conversation. You also told me that we would talk about it later during our next game of chess. I surely hope that you would believe that you can trust me and that I am here for you no matter what the situation or circumstance is." Mr. Robinson was right. He has always been in my corner and supported me in all my endeavors. Some he agreed with and some he didn't. I can remember a lot of cases to when mother would recommend that I have a talk with Mr. Robinson. He has always been a big part of my life, kind of like a second parent. I guess it may have been because he was the only black male in my life that I could ever be able to identify with coming up in this town. I guess a talk with Mr. Robinson might not be bad after all.

"Being black and having a white mother never really bothered me as much as it did the day Kira met Mother. It made me truly take a closer look at my life and how I was brought up in this world. I started to feel like I didn't belong here and that everyone was just giving me pity instead of love and friendship. It's not every day you see an abandoned black child raised by a white family. For once in my life, I felt alone with no sign or trace of my parents. How could two people do such a thing? I really hope they never feel any peace after what they have done. If I met them today, I wouldn't have any words for them, only hatred." The game had stopped and the moment seemed to stand still. Mr. Robinson put the chess piece back on the board and began to focus on me.

"Hating someone won't solve your issue. It will only create bitterness; bitterness that could harm you and your future relationships with others. I wasn't abandoned by my parents like you were but we do have similar cases. I hated my father throughout my school years. The McCormics helped me overcome my bitterness and hatred. Mrs. McCormic had shown me how my hatred for my father was affecting me in my athletics, my academics, and my personal relationships with others. I never saw my mother again. My hatred for my father had consumed me to the point to where even God and I were not on speaking terms. He eventually drank himself to death. I never attended his funeral, nor did I ever go to see him in the hospital before his death. The McCormics tried to persuade me in a different direction, but I wouldn't hear of it. I stayed in college and never came home. My animosity toward my parents started influencing decisions I would make and determining the coarse I would choose to take. Bitterness and hatred started eating at me from the inside out. Once I had learned to love and forgive my parents, I was able to advance in life and grow as a better man. Though neither of them was around to hear me say that I forgive them, I myself was free. Bitterness and hatred toward another person has no effect on anyone, but the person that it has set root in. They neither condemn, nor hinder the person on which they are targeted. Anger and bitterness just affect the host in whom they take root. Don't get me wrong, there are some mistakes that I have made in the past that I wish I could alter but we cannot erase what has been written in time. Would it make you feel any different if they had died and you were adopted? What if they were here now and explained to you the reason you were raised by the

McCormics? What if they did love you and just couldn't give you the life you deserved, so they gave you up to people who could? Would that make you feel better?" Mr. Robinson was reminding me of the talk Kira and I had the day she met mother. I began to notice how I had been treating mother and my friends once I had become angry.

He and Kira were right. In such anger I had hurt my mother that day and started pushing away my best friends. "Funny, Kira said something similar," laughing as I responded.

"Then she must be a special woman. It takes a lot to keep from hating those who have wronged us or caused pain in our lives. It's not easy son. I have watched you from the moment you were brought into this world. God has given you a wonderful life and you have turned out to be a fine young man. I am and will always be proud of you and thankful to be so privileged to have been a major part of your life." Mr. Robinson always knew what to say. He always had the right words for the situation. He was right; we all have had our share of faults in the past. We should do our best to never lay judgment on those who make mistakes.

"So tell me more about the lovely Kira. I was able to get a better look at her when she came to visit you at the nursing home. She doesn't look like most of the girls you have dated in the past." Mr. Robinson was changing the mood by making me talk about Kira. He knew I was into her and it would bring a better mood to the room. As we played and I continued to lose, I had realized that these chess games were merely quality time spent with him and me. It didn't matter who won or lost, just as long as we were able to have a good relationship.

"I met Kira a while back at the high school rival football game. I stumbled upon her as I was looking for a seat in the stands. Funny how things happen; she was there alone watching her niece cheerlead for Highland. The little girl was quite a natural.

"You know those games are always cold to watch. Kira was next to me shivering and talking to herself. I overheard her and offered her a spare blanket that I had with me. I called myself being a gentleman. Next thing I knew, we were at Alice's having milkshakes and dessert."

"Well, that does seem like a nice place to have met a woman. She was there watching her niece? Who are her folks? Do we know them? Do they live here in town?" Out of all the people I had asked about Kira, I had never thought to ask Mr. Robinson. I'm sure he wouldn't know anything about the Alexanders having any children as well.

"She said her parents are Mr. and Mrs. Alexander. You know that rich couple. They live on the outskirts of town? The Mr. Alexander that rarely goes out in public unless it's to get Mrs. Alexanders medicine." Mr. Robinson made his move then reared back in his chair resting both elbows on the arms, folding his hands together.

"I don't recall the Alexanders birthing any children. Did you tell your mother about the Alexanders being her parents? What did she have to say?"

"Mother and everyone else couldn't recall the Alexanders having any children as well. I haven't had a chance to meet her parents yet but I do find the story a little strange, being that no one recalls them having any children."

"Well, I don't think they were always that way. I can't recall the incident but something happened to that family that caused them to be so withheld. Mr. and Mrs. McCormic knew about it along with few of the more upscale town's people. I will certainly have to talk to Mrs. Brenda in the morning when I go in to work. Well, I have to go son. I have a few errands to run while I'm off today. Meanwhile, tomorrow I will be sure to ask your mother about what may have happened in the past with the Alexanders. It is always a pleasure having someone on one time with you while whipping up on you in a couple games of chess."

After he put his coat and hat on, he gave me a hug and walked out the door. I watched from the living room window as he made his way to his truck. He gave one last wave and a smile before he got in his truck and pulled off. Even though Mr. Robinson couldn't recall the issue I felt as though I might be getting somewhere with this mysterious Kira Alexander. I couldn't stop thinking of what could have happened to make the Alexanders so withheld. I understand that losing both a daughter and a son in law in the same day could cause some damage but what remains a mystery is the birth of Kira and her sister. No one knows them or recalls the Alexanders having any kids. Even if they did not originate in this town, there is no story of them moving here with any children. Maybe they moved when the girls had already been born and moved off to private school. This is truly something that will be stuck on my brain until I find some sort of answer or clarity.

I thought to call up Trent to meet me at the Hole in the Wall for some football and wings, but all I got was the voicemail when I called. So I decided that I was going to run a few errands, then go alone, eat some wings, and watch a little college football. It may be a good thing to spend the day alone after all. After the talk Mr. Robinson and I had, I needed time to clear my thoughts and not focus so much on the case with Kira.

Like every Saturday afternoon during football season, the place was packed. I found a small booth next to our normal seating area in the rear of the restaurant. Once I had gotten good and situated, I ordered a small pizza, wings, and a tall glass of Dr. Pepper.

"Hey, cousin, where are the rest of the musketeers?" It was Jacs and few other women that I had never met. I assume they may be some of her co-workers from the clinic, being that Jacs was still in her work attire.

"Oh, I'm dining alone today. I had just got done playing chess back at the house with Mr. Robinson. What brings you here?" I asked as I looked around her to observe her company that she arrived with.

"Things were a little slow today at the clinic, so the girls and I had gotten off work a little early. We decided to grab something to eat together before we all went home. We didn't want anything fancy. I suggested that we come here and unwind. Mr. Robinson, huh? I remember good ole Mr. Robinson. How has he been?" Jacs sat down for a second while her friends proceeded to be seated a few booths down from where I was located.

"Mr. Robinson is doing well, still working as the head maintenance man at the nursing home, and always giving me 'fatherly advice' as usual. We had a good chitchat today. I had just finished running some errands before I came here. Some of the things we had talked about were still on the brain. I didn't want to spend the rest of my day pondering on questions and mysteries that I had no solution to. So I figured that some pizza, wings, and sports would be a good way to enjoy the rest of my day off."

"Any of those issues similar to the one we discussed over lunch a couple weeks ago?"

"No, these are a little different. I don't really have the answers and there isn't really much solution into talking about it to others. It's about Kira and why no one knows her or where she really came from. As Mr. Robinson and I were talking today, he had a bit of information on the Alexanders that may be able to piece together this puzzle. The problem is that he just couldn't remember exactly what it was. Jacs, don't let me keep you occupied from your friends with my troubles. You go on and enjoy the rest of the day with your girlfriends."

"Kyle, are you sure you don't want me to sit here with you?" Jacs was always a caring individual. It didn't matter what it was that she could be doing, it was never nothing too great to keep her from being in my corner.

"Yes. Besides, I only ordered enough pizza and wings for myself. I sure don't need you digging your paws in it." She and I both got a big laugh out of that comment as she was getting up to go join her friends. She put her hand on my shoulder, leaned over, kissed me on the forehead, and went to where her girls were seated.

A little while after my food arrived and I started to dig in, my phone started to ring. It was Kira. She said that she didn't really want anything, just that she was thinking about me and wanted to hear my voice. She said that she and her niece were out of town shopping today. I told her about Mr. Robinson coming by but not what we had discussed, how I ran a few errands, and now sitting here at the Hole in the Wall. I invited her over after work tomorrow for dinner and a drink. She replied with "Gladly!" Before we hung up with each other, she said she missed me and couldn't wait to see me. It felt good to hear that from her, especially having the feelings I had the night of the wedding. I am still a little concerned about her history but not to where whatever it is will turn me away. I, too, was anxious to see her tomorrow. After we hung up, I boxed up what I couldn't finish to go, waved goodbye to Jacs, and headed home for the rest of the day.

CHAPTER SEVEN

The next day at work wasn't so busy. I finished up what little paperwork that I had and then headed to my mother's living quarters for a visit. When I had arrived at her room, she was in the kitchen as usual.

"Hi, honey, so good to see you today! How was your weekend?" She came and greeted me with a hug as we went into the living room. I could tell she was in a good mood today as she sat down beside me. She had a beautiful glow about her that I couldn't quite describe, on top of the smell of brownies baking throughout her quarters.

"My weekend was great." I assume she meant anything that happened after the wedding and the reception. "Mr. Robinson had stopped by about midafternoon yesterday. He and I played a few games of chess, listened to our old record, and had a deep conversation." Speaking of Mr. Robinson, he said he was going to ask mother about the Alexanders. "Mother, Mr. Robinson didn't stop by today by any chance, did he?"

"No, dear, I believe one of the maintenance men are out on sick leave today. They were having some electrical issues over in the west wing. One of the girls was talking about it during our get together for breakfast this morning. You two and your time together bless me. It is always good to know that you two are so close. I'm glad you guys are able to have a relationship. You know that he loves and adores you? He has been in your life since you were born. He took to you as soon as we brought you home. I believe your presence in his life has made him the wonderful man that he is today." Mr. Robinson was truly a great friend of the family. I guess she was so happy about our relationship because he was the only black male in my life and it would make me feel not so alone. Mr. Robison has always been there indeed, like a young second father figure of some sort.

"Yes, I know mother. I wonder if I would have seen him on television playing professional basketball if he hadn't messed up his knee and lost his scholarship."

"I had almost forgotten about his knee injury. He had gotten hurt a little while before you were born. I remember how worried and depressed he was. It took some time before Kenneth and I could get him to come back around and pick himself back up. He was worried sick about how he was going to make a living. Before his injury, he had big plans to show us how thankful he was. He used to tell Kenneth how he was going to buy him a brand new motorcycle as a gift for all he had done. He was going to buy me this pearl necklace that I wear every day. Your father had told him I loved pearls, so this was his big gift to me. After things started looking better for John, and life seemed to be okay, Kenneth started to get sick. John never was able to buy Kenneth that motorcycle and give it to him, so he bought it for himself. He bought this for me shortly after Kenneth passed," she said as she was fingering the pearls around her neck.

"Is Mr. Robinson's mother still alive?"

"No. I don't believe he ever found his mother. To show his forgiveness, John bought his father's old house and now rents it out on the south side of town. He has quite a few rental properties all over town." Mr. Robinson never told me about the rental property, but it sure does sound like he is doing well for himself. Then again, most of the time we spend together, he is always asking about me and my life. I guess I never really stopped to ask him about what was going on with him and his life.

We had talked so much about Mr. Robinson that I had lost track of time and had to get back to work. I gave my mother a hug and a kiss and hurried back to my office. While I was going down the hallway, I had thought to myself that I had never got to mention anything about Kira, nor anything about mine and Mr. Robinson's conversation over the Alexanders. I had intentions on traveling to the west wing to see Mr. Robinson, but I was short on time to finish what work I had left. Plus, I had an appointment with a brother and sister that were thinking about admitting their aunt. Not to mention that I had to get home and prepare for my dinner date with Kira. This will be the first time that she has ever been to my house and I really want to make an outstanding impression.

On the way home, I had stopped to pick up some groceries and a bottle wine. I wanted things to be nice and simple. We had been on a few dates already, so I wanted her to feel comfortable as though she and I have been together for a while. Once I got home, I tidied up a little bit, and took a quick shower while dinner was being prepared. I had lit the fireplace in the living room and some candles throughout the house. It wasn't long before I heard a car door outside in the driveway. I met Kira at the door to let her in. Dinner wasn't ready yet, but I poured her and myself a drink as we stood in the kitchen talking.

"How was your day yesterday?" she asked as we sat on the stools at the island in the kitchen.

"Quiet, I ran some errands and spent a little time to myself. I did get to do some catching up with Mr. Robinson as well." I had forgotten that Kira had never even met Mr. Robinson. I reckon this is the first time that I have ever mentioned his name around her.

"Mr. Robinson?" she asked.

"Yes, he is head of maintenance at the nursing home. He is also a real close friend of the family. I have known him since I was born. He is the only black male in my life that I know personally. He kind of had it rough growing up when he was younger as well. His mom abandoned him to his father. His father didn't care for him too much neither, so my parents took him in and raised him. He and I have a close relationship. He has been a great influence on my life and always there for me like a father."

"Like a father, huh? Sounds like your parents have been a blessing to more than one or two people throughout their life. You truly have a nice family. I am really glad I met your mother. She also made me feel like one of the family at the wedding. Marcus and Jacs made me feel welcome as well. It seemed like everybody just made it easy for me to fit in."

"Well, I am truly glad to hear that. My family is special. I must say that there is a lot of love within the McCormic family. I think part of that is because they know how I feel about you as well. From the time I met you at the high school up until the wedding, you were all I talked about around my friends. How was your day with your niece?"

"We had a blast. We went out of town to go shopping. We shopped all day, had dinner, and then went to the movies. We ended up staying at this expensive hotel. I ended up getting us a suite. We had pillow fights, swam, and ate room service all night and most of the next day. I took her to the spa once we got home. She had fun, but I think I really needed the relaxation and fun myself."

"Sounds like you two did have a nice time. Somewhat of a vacation it seems like. I can't wait to meet her and your parents." There it was—the set up to have an important discussion.

"Sure that would be nice. Maybe we all can go to an amusement park or a small trip to Alice's. Yum, something sure smells delicious. You think dinner is ready?" I could tell that she was trying to get off the subject of meeting her family by how quick she changed the subject, and how she immediately left her stool to head to the stove.

"Yes, I hope you like lasagna? I wanted today to be simple, so I didn't make anything too special. It's one of those lasagnas you buy at the store already made and just throw in the oven." I followed her to the stove and removed the lasagna. I fixed our plates, poured us some more wine, and lead her to the dining room. She followed with the bread and wine. She seated herself next to me at the table. Seemed weird not sitting across from each other but I did enjoy her being close to me.

"Kyle, this is delicious. Wow, a man that knows his way around the kitchen. I'm impressed. There aren't many men that are sweet, ambitious, handsome, career and family oriented that can cook also. I'm curious to what the flaw or catch is to why there is no wife or girl-friend?" I could sense her sarcasm over the store bought lasagna, but all the other things she said I'm sure are true. She had been successful in completely changing the subject to get me away from asking more questions about her family.

"I guess I just never felt like I have found that special one until right now. I don't really date all that much. I'm a bit of somewhat shy.

I really don't approach women and not a lot of women approach me. I really don't know how long it has been since I have dated anyone. To be honest, you are the first girl that I have brought to my house or had met my mother since I have been out of college. Normally, women don't last to make it to the second or third date."

"I will take that as me being one of a kind or special by the sound of that. Kyle, I think you are a great guy. Too good to be true at times but I can't help myself. I am truly interested in where this could go or what we could be. I hope I don't scare you away when I say this but it has been a while since I have dated also. The last guy I dated, I thought he had it all together. I was really head over hills for him. Once he knew he had my heart, he started placing me under all these rules, picking and choosing where I could go, and who I could hang out with. At first, we did everything as far as dating and trips and then it all stopped. He stopped being affectionate and didn't want any affection from me. He didn't cheat on me or anything. He was just controlling toward the end. I was a teacher when he and I were together. I started taking an interest in physical fitness and nutrition. I came home one day and expressed how I was interested in the profession. All I can say is that he wasn't so supportive of my career move. I had called myself being a good woman and trying to keep our relationship together. We had a deep discussion one day. It was supposed to be some give and take or some sort of a compromise. As I think about it now, it was a contract negotiation for a concession on my part. In which, later wasn't enough and he wanted more. I couldn't give up anymore or change. I became miserable and eventually moved out." We ate, she talked, as I listened. We ended up in the living room on the couch watching a movie on television. We had finished the first bottle of wine. I had opened another bottle while we talked. Before I knew it we had dozed off on the couch.

When I had awaken the next morning, we were still on the couch under the blanket that I keep on the back of my couch for nights when the fellas were too drunk to drive home. She was lying on top of me with her head on my chest. She felt good in my arms. The smell of her hair was one thing that caught my attention while she was still lying on my chest. A little bit after I had awoken, her head had finally started to rise.

"Wow, we must have nodded off. I guess we may have had a little too much to drink," I said as she was waking up. Once she came to, she scooted up a little further and we started passionately kissing there on the couch. I wasn't going to try anything. I just caressed her body as I enjoyed her lips pressed against mine. Although I would love for us to go upstairs to my room, it was too soon. My feelings for her were above us going to my bed for some morning sex. I didn't want to come on too strong and it was important to me how she felt and what she thought of me. Once our lips departed, her beautiful eyes were gazing into mine.

"I had a good time spending last night with you. Baby, I have got to go. Plus, I'm sure you are late for work yourself." She smiled as she was getting up from lying on top of me. Heck, work was the last thing on my mind. I would have called in to spend most of my day with company and a moment like this. She slid on her shoes, grabbed her coat, put her hair up, and I walked her to the door. "Call me later." She kissed me passionately once more before she headed to her car.

I went upstairs and turned on the shower. Goodness that felt good to wake up with her still here. I had her scent all over me and didn't want to wash it off. Our kiss on the couch kept replaying over and over in my mind. At this point, I was on cloud nine and so emotionally high from last night that I absolutely did not want to go to work today or tomorrow even. At this point, Kira is everything that I want in a woman. I had loved everything about her up to now. While getting ready to go to work, all I could think about was the first night we met, Alice's, the day she returned the blanket, when she met mother, the wedding, and last night. I called Kira on my way to work. She was in the shower when I called. I told her that I didn't mean to bother her, but I just had to hear her voice after her overnight visit and how I felt about waking up to her this morning. She too, told me how good it felt and how wonderful she thought things were going. She and I both talked about how it felt as though this was naturally unfolding. We were getting along—attracted to each other, and enjoying the time we were spending.

As we talked, I could picture her smiling on the other end of the phone while she was getting ready. Once I arrived at work and before we hung up, she told me she missed me and couldn't wait to see me again.

I was walking pass the front office, when I was stopped by Mrs. Sharon. I noticed she wasn't at her desk when I had grabbed my paperwork. I had thought to myself that I had surely slipped by her unnoticed, by being so late. "Did someone have a long night last night Mr. McCormic?" My back was to her, but I could hear the laughter in her voice. She had caught me by surprise, stopping me in my tracks.

"Yes, it was, Mrs. Sharon, but not long enough," I replied as I looked back with a smile and winked at her.

I was really late this morning. I'm normally on my way to see my mother for lunch by this time. I had gathered a few things to work on from the office and headed off to see my mother. Today, there was pep in my step and music in my head. I was truly happy with what was going on in my life.

Once I arrived at Mother's living quarters, the door was slightly cracked and you could smell coffee brewing. She was sitting on the couch talking to Mr. Robinson as I entered.

"Hello, dear!" She rose to her feet, greeting me with a hug and kiss before I sat down.

"Hello, son! I had come by your office today before I came to see your mother but you were nowhere to be found. Mrs. Sharon said she hadn't seen you and your car was not in the parking lot. Is everything all right?"

"Yes, sir, everything is wonderful," I replied with a smile on my face, hoping someone would ask me what I seemed so happy about today.

"Why, you sure seem to be full of life today. Do tell us what has brought about such a glow on my boy's face today?" I knew I could count on my mother to be curious about what was going on.

"I had a wonderful night last night. Kira and I had dinner at the old house. We drank a couple bottles of wine while watching TV and sharing some conversation. I guess we must have had too much to drink because she woke up in my arms this morning. Last night and this morning are to be one of the best moments in my life."

"You two didn't?" My mother paused before she finished the rest of the question with her hand over chest in concern.

"No, Mother. Neither took advantage of the other. Although the kiss we shared this morning was wonderful. I must admit, I was so high off of her and full of passion that I didn't feel like coming to work today."

"Speaking of Kira, your mother and I were just discussing the Alexanders before you arrived," Mr. Robinson interrupted.

"Yes, dear. Has she ever told you anything about her parents?"

I didn't give them all the information because I was concerned if Kira may have been hiding something from me. Some bad news would just crush my spirits with the way I was feeling at this moment. "Nothing more than her parents living off their wealth, and out in the suburbs on the outskirts of town. Why, is there something wrong?"

"John and I were just trying to recall an incident years ago concerning the Alexanders. Rumor had it that Mr. and Mrs. Alexander had a child that was shipped away to a private school upstate. I believe you and your friends were starting your second or third year of high school at the time this happened. Rumor has it that once the teenage girl had briefly arrived in town, she was pregnant with child. Being that Mr. Alexander had never wanted children in the first place, the teenage girl was shipped off to an all-girls school upstate after she gave birth. The Alexanders have been raising this child while her mother was off in school. They say that Mrs. Alexander insisted on raising the child and forcing the teenage mother to finish high school and further her education. Strange thing is that the girl never returned. Kyle, does Kira have any children?" I tried my best to not change my expression on my face. A pit was forming in my stomach and a knot followed in my throat. I was hoping that my mother's old age was causing her to get the story mixed up. Today had started off wonderful and as I was about to climax, I am being grounded by such news.

"No, she hadn't mentioned anything about having any children." I couldn't remember if I had told mother or Mr. Robinson that Kira was at the game watching her niece cheer the night we met. I just didn't know how to respond or what to say at this moment. I was quiet, the whole room was quiet. Mother and Mr. Robinson were fixed on me as I was in deep thought and floored by the news. What if mother was right? Did Kira abandon her child the same way I was abandoned? Could they have been talking about her sister being forced to abandon her daughter and then come back after school was finished? All I could do was reflect on the walk we had after Kira met my mother and heard my life story. It almost would explain her opinion on keeping a close eye to make sure the child was okay. Part of me was hoping Mother was wrong, the other half just was in shambles and confused on what to think about Kira. To me she had been the most wonderful woman I had ever met and wanting to pursue things, possibly the one I wanted to spend the rest of my life with. After hearing such a story from my mother, I felt as though she could have been lying to me the whole time. Why would she lie? I had been going through enough already and now this story has come to light.

Then the silence was broken by Mr. Robinson. "Son, are you okay? Speak what is on your mind. I know this isn't the news you expected to hear, so say what is on your mind."

"I don't know what to say, sir. Obviously I don't know too much about her except for the last few weeks that she and I have been dating."

Out of embarrassment, I left the room without saying goodbye to anyone. At this moment, I felt like everything was a lie. I felt as though Kira had been putting on this facade the whole time. How was I to get the truth out of her? As I walked in my office, I had closed the door in behind me. I sat there in silence; replaying the night of the football game over and over in my head, trying to envision the resemblance between Kira and her niece. Also wondering how she could sit there and tell such a lie and smile at the same time. It all makes sense to what she said to me about keeping a close eye to make sure the child was okay. She was keeping her distance from Chelsie, by hiding behind the role of an aunt. It explains why they do so much and she is so into her niece. What a dirty thing to do to someone. She sat there and told me this lie with a smile on her face like there was no wrong in the whole story. I was hoping that the news I had heard wasn't true, but if it is, then she should be ashamed. By this time, I was racking my brain trying to figure out how I was going to meet Chelsie and the Alexanders. I wanted the truth!

Then I heard a knock at the door before it opened. It was Mr. Robinson. "Are you okay? I know there is a lot on your mind. It would be better to get it off, so please tell me what you are thinking?"

He was right. I was about to explode with so much running through my mind. "How could she lie? This whole thing has been a lie. When I met her at the football game, she said she was there to watch her niece. Her niece in which, I assume is her daughter by the story my mother just told me less than an hour ago. What would you do if you were in my shoes?" I was hoping that whatever he was going to respond with would ease the situation.

"If I were you, I would get the truth before I reacted. I believe everything in life happens for a reason and the decisions we are led to make have an influence behind them. Yes, get the truth, but try to put yourself in her shoes also. Try to understand why things were handled the way they were. Just because she may have traveled a rough road in life does not make her a bad person. We all have our flaws and mistakes son. Lord knows that I have made my share of messes along with trying to fix them. Continue to see her for the person you thought she was before you heard what you just heard back there. I'm sure she likes you, and coming right out with her life story would not have led you to the relationship you two have today. It is easy to judge, pour out anger, and hurt others. If you can find it in you, try to help her, not hurt her. You are a good man son, I am sure you will do the right thing. Just take some time to think things through before you make a decision. Trust me on this one." Mr. Robinson then turned and walked out the door.

Not long after he left, I had gathered my things to head home. I was high off the romance we shared from last night up until I met mother and Mr. Robinson this morning. The story I had heard from mother took away the music, clouds, and butterflies, leaving me with chronic pain and sickness. I felt lied to. I know no one is perfect, but are there necessary situations in which lies are accepted? Instead of being so anxious to see Kira again, I needed time away to clear my head. Mr. Robinson was right; a bad past does not make her a bad person. I can't say I don't understand why she didn't tell me neither. I am sure she is still holding on to that shame. A part of me says I shouldn't even bother with it, dump her, and get on with my life. A great deal of me wants to help her. I felt like I needed someone to talk to, but who? I wouldn't share this information with just anybody. I was feeling somewhat embarrassed that I had fallen for someone with such a story. Before I could make it home, I turned around and headed back to the nursing home. The only person I could talk to about it and share my feelings with is my mother.

Once I arrived and started through the doors, I met Mr. Robinson on his way out. "Back so soon, son?"

"Yes, sir, I forgot something in my office." I kept walking as I thought of some quick lie so he wouldn't hold me up with any questions concerning my feelings about Kira.

I quickly made my way to my mother's living quarters. The door was slightly opened as usual. I gave it a small knock, pushing it open as I entered her domain. "Hello, Mother." She was on the couch in her living room. I could tell she was working on another photo album. On the coffee table was the box of photos and the album she took from the house the day we went to the wedding rehearsal. She immediately put it away as I was walking toward the couch.

"Aren't you off work now, dear? What brings you back so unexpected?"

"I left without talking to you about the story I heard this morning. I can't stop thinking about it. I felt that Kira was the one up until now. Now I don't know what to do about her. Everything was working itself out so perfectly at first." I just wanted to fall into my mother's arms and cry. I honestly felt like a fool.

She placed her hand on my knee as I sat down beside her. "Why are things falling apart now? Just because you heard of her past, that you aren't for certain about what happened and don't have the absolute truth? That does not make her a liar or a bad person. Nor does it mean she has been putting on a facade this whole time. I'm sure that girl is genuine in her feelings toward you. I am sure she may carry a little shame in where her life is right now. I know she really likes you Kyle. I could tell at the wedding and that day she showed up here at your job. Nothing is a lie or fake about her feelings toward you. Does it bother you that she may have a child? Could your feelings about this come from how you were raised? Put yourself in her shoes! Here is this handsome man showing a lot of interest in me; should I start off by telling him about my horrific past?"

Mother made a valid point. "I have never dated a woman with a child before but I don't think that would be a problem. I think I could handle that much. I guess some of the ill feelings come from the life that I have lived. At least one parent is a part of that little girl's life."

"Honey, do your mother a favor? You're a good man and if you are falling in love with Kira, try to be there for her? Give it a chance first, and if it doesn't work out between the two of you, then you know. Don't let it be because of some awful thing that happened to her years ago. If the story happens to be remotely true, then I am sure she has been turned away all of her life. I can't imagine how life has been for her all along. Just to think about all she has been through makes me feel sorry for the poor girl. I couldn't imagine being torn from you, Kyle. I'm sure there are some deep hurts and scares she is dealing with. I couldn't fathom how a person could keep all of that hurt and pain bottled up for all these years. I'm sure she just needs someone to give her a chance, and some encouragement. I think she may have found that in you."

"So you're saying I should be a superman or treat this like some charity case?" That was a harsh way of putting it but that was the message I was receiving.

"No. I'm telling you not to miss out on what could be a beautiful thing in the end because of how that situation looks now. Make sure you find out for yourself if it is truly worth letting go. If she has moved back to the town, then I am sure she is trying to establish a setting for her to have a better relationship with her daughter if that be the case. I can only imagine how hard it must be, wanting to tell the truth for the better, hoping you don't get rejected for the worst.

What if your mother or father were out there somewhere wishing they could do the same with you? How would you respond? How do you think they would feel if you were to just reject them? I know you have been feeling rejected by them here lately, but there are things in life that influence the decisions we make and have made in the past. Not to say that we always make the right decisions, but don't let hatred and bitterness set root in your heart son." Mother was making sense. I could tell her and dad had this talk many times in life, because Mr. Robinson had given me the same advice. I guess you could say that he listened. I don't know if I could accept my mother or father popping up in my life at this moment trying to make amends. I couldn't forgive them right now for abandoning me.

"Mother, what if you are right? Maybe her niece is her daughter and her moving back to town may be her setting the stage for the truth to come out. I don't even know how I could help her if she doesn't tell me the truth or even let me meet her parents. Do you think if she let me meet her parents that they would tell me the whole story? Maybe that is why I haven't been around Chelsie? Kira is afraid that I might see the resemblance even though she said she had a twin sister. How could I get the truth out of Kira?"

"Patience, my son, when she is ready to tell you or rely on you for help, I'm sure she will let you know. Keep things going the way they are currently progressing at this moment, I'm sure the time will come when things will surface. Don't force anything with meeting her parents. The last thing you want for her to experience is you finding out the truth through another source. You need to clear your thoughts and be ready to react. I'm not trying to force you to keep her or help her. I just think she is a good woman that may be trying to fix what was once wrong. There is nothing wrong with a mother going after her child. I admire anyone who admits a mistake and tries to correct it. It's not easy." Mother was right. Aside from the story I heard today, I still had feelings for Kira. I am glad I came back and had a talk with my mother. I may have made a mess of things with Kira if she had called and I had talked to her before having this talk with mother. I am willing to let things take their coarse, but part of me is ready to dive into the truth and work on straightening things out, if I can help. I hope the best for Kira and that she will open up to me about it soon if all this is true. I hope Chelsie receives her with open arms and doesn't reject her. I know it would kill Kira to lose what relationship they have now.

"I see your point, Mother, and you are right. I should not let Kira's past dictate my feelings for the person she is today, especially not knowing the truth. I will continue to date and let our relation-ship grow. I am glad that I came back to talk with you. There is no telling how I may have reacted if I had talked to Kira with this on my mind or before you and I could have a heart to heart. You and Mr. Robinson had the same advice in mind." I have always counted on Mr. Robinson and my parents for guidance and advice. Things are going great with Kira and me. I would love them to progress but in the back of my mind there are questions lying in wait to be answered.

I then hugged and kissed my mother goodbye. I barely waved or spoke to anybody as I was walking out of the nursing home. I had so many things running through my mind; I couldn't acknowledge the things or people that were in my path. Once I had gotten in my car, my phone had begun to ring. It was Trent calling for everyone to meet up at the Hole in the Wall tonight. I told him that I would be there after I went home and took a quick shower.

While on the way home, I couldn't get Kira off my mind. So I picked up my phone and called her. Wonder what she is doing tonight. I should invite her out with us.

"Hello, this is Kira."

"Hey, I was wondering if you had any plans tonight. The guys and I were going out for wings, drinks, and watch a game or two. You busy?"

"Uh, no, not that I can think of. Let me finish with Chelsie, get cleaned up, get dressed, and I will be on my way. Sound like a plan, dear?"

"That will be great, you can meet me at my house and I will drive us there, if that would be fine with you?"

"That would be great, I don't need to dress up or anything, do I?"

"No, just dress comfortable."

"Okay, Mr. McCormic, I will see you in about forty-five minutes," with smile and giggle in her voice as she replied before hanging up.

I was pulling in the driveway as we were hanging up. The deep thoughts and questions had put themselves on hold as I had heard Kira's voice in our quick conversation. I really like this girl and I hope that things will not have any effect on our relationship once they surface. If Chelsie truly is her daughter and reunite in all she is trying to do, then I hope things go smoothly. I really do hate how things unfolded, but I hope it gets better for Kira. Maybe one day, I can meet, and get along with her parents.

It didn't take long to shower, throw on some jeans, and a sweat shirt. Before I knew it, there was a knock at the door, it was Kira. She came in for a second as I rounded up my keys, coat, and wallet. It wasn't that cold out to me, but I grabbed my coat in case she may need to borrow it. The ride into town was pretty smooth. We talked about how both of our days went. She spent most of the day with Chelsie. Questions and the eagerness for a confession spun in the back of my mind the whole time she talked about her "niece." By the way she talks of her, you could tell the two of them have a strong bond and she really adores the child.

Once we arrived, Marcus, Jacs, and Trent were outside waiting. They all greeted Kira with a hug before we entered the sports bar. The host asked us for our usual table as she escorted us through the crowd. Game nights were always crowded at the Hole in the Wall. As the guys and I had become regulars, all the hosts would do their best to keep from seating customers in our area. As we were seated at our table, Jacs and Marcus sat across from me and Kira, Trent seated himself at the head. As we sat down, Jac's eyes followed Kira as she scooted her chair closer to mine. Jac's then turned and winked at me. I really liked Kira. It felt great to sense how into our relationship she was. Although, with all the news going on; there is still a part of me that feels kind of uncomfortable with all the missing pieces to the puzzle. I just hope we don't get in too deep and things fall apart because of her personal issue and untold story.

"Marcus and I were thinking about a mini vacation in the mountains for this winter, nothing too spectacular or fancy. Just to get away somewhere off in a cabin. Get a cabin for two or three days—nothing but a cabin, fireplace, and maybe an indoor hot tub?" Jacs had a nice idea I will admit. It would be nice to get away from this town for a little bit with all I have going on and the issue with Kira.

Trent was the next to respond. "Sounds like a great idea, Jacs. We haven't been to the mountains since college. I'm sure I can scroll through my phone and find someone to tag along."

"Oh, Lord. I remember the last time we went and you had someone tag along. She got drunk, broke a lamp, and puked all over the place. I bet that area still reeks with the smell of vomit. Now that you mention it, you still owe me for having to replace the lamp the little tramp broke," laughing as she replied to Trent's comment.

Before I could speak, Kira voiced her opinion. "I think that could be nice. I have never been in a cabin or in the mountains for the most part. I have been in need of a little vacation and excitement in my life". She then looked a Jacs with a big smile of sarcasm and said, "I wouldn't be one of Mr. McCormic's little embarrassing tramps now, would I?"

Trent with an outburst of laughter added, "No, not at all. Kyle never really brought any females around us. I to this day would find question in asking did he ever date anyone. He always had a friend or two but nothing serious. Tonight is actually a little special because you are the first woman he has brought around us." Way to go Trent. Way to make me look like a lame. It was somewhat true. I never truly brought anyone around my friend although I did have potential mates in college. I just never really had that feeling of "she could be the one" or "this is the game changer" with anyone.

"I think that is a great idea, Jacs. We should have a four day weekend in the mountains. You guys get everything worked out, give everyone a date, and we all can plan a small mini vacation. I'm definitely game." Even with all the issues I secretly had with Kira, I was still somewhat confident that things were okay to go ahead with the idea of this mini vacation. I wanted to stop thinking about what could be the truth and what could be a lie with Kira. The thoughts rolling around in my head started making it harder to enjoy time spent with her. I noticed how I was starting to decipher everything she was saying. Besides, Mom and Mr. Robinson told me not to act any different.

The waitress came, took our order, and the conversation was non-stop. The guys talked about sports and work, while Jacs and Kira scooted down a bit for their own conversation. Jacs was always good about making people feel welcome and no one being left out when it came to females mingling with the group. Although, she did give Trent the full report after the night was over. She would definitely let him know whether the girl he brought was a keeper or not. I can't say they were all bad. Trent's playboy behavior has caused him to pass up some good women in the past as well. Once again, Kira was the first to come around the team to my knowledge. I admit that it did feel kind of strange watching her get interviewed by Jacs. I hope she passes. For the most part, Kira seemed to have fit right in with the group tonight. She acted as though she had been a part of the group as long as the four of us have known each other. I had felt comfortable around her. By the why she responded to the idea of a mini vacation, you could tell she had gotten a little comfortable with me. It will be a first time for us both; her first time in the mountains and my first time on vacation with a date.

When we were done, we all walked out to our vehicles together. The fellas and I bid our farewell, Kira and Jacs hugged each other goodbye. As they were hugging each other, Jacs had given a wink and smile. I assumed everything checked out fine. With the issues slowly minimizing themselves, I was becoming more confident that things were fine. I was a little proud of my first time bringing a female out with the crew.

On the ride back to my house, all Kira did was talk about Jacs. How she liked her as a person and how comfortable she felt talking to her. She told me that they exchanged numbers at the table and made plans to do lunch sometime in the near future. She said they were very much a like growing up as far as their love for sports. She said she also participated in track, softball, and soccer. She went on to tell me about how she had a college scholarship in softball as well. Only that she played out east opposed to Jacs playing out west. She told me education was her major in college and nutrition was her minor. It reminded me of her taking on a teaching job here in town to be closer to Chelsie and the rest of her family. Before I could ask, she said all of the teaching spots had been filled for this year. She was only a substitute for this school year and that she was told that she would be full time next year. She said that five spots would be available due to five teachers retiring after this school year.

Once we pulled up in the driveway, we sat in the car for a couple of minutes.

"It has gotten pretty late. Do you mind if I just crash here for the night? I know you work in the morning, I won't bother you." I could never say no to her sweetness and beauty. Plus, I felt that tonight went so well, why not.

"Sure, there are plenty of spare rooms in the house. Take your pick and I will find you something to sleep in," I replied. It was a five bedroom house. My folks had left it to me. Ever since I have moved in, I don't think I had anyone spend the night but the fellas and Jacs.

As we entered the house, I asked Kira what would be most comfortable for her to sleep in? She said, "Show me your closet. Surely I can find something to wear in there myself."

"As you top the stairs, you will find the master bedroom on your left. There is a walk-in closet in my bedroom. Maybe you will find something in there to wear. I'm going to head to the kitchen and grab us something to drink while you change." I proceeded to the kitchen as she went up the stairs. I had grabbed a bottle of wine and two glasses, and sat at the island in the kitchen. After I had corked the bottle and was getting ready to pour, I could hear Kira coming down the stairs.

"Did you find anything to your liking up there, dear?"

"Yes, I hope you don't mind me wearing one of your work shirts? You had plenty to choose from but I think I like this one the most." She had on one of my powder blue, long sleeved, button down shirts that I wear to work with some old gray sweat pants on. Although the cloths were a bit big on her, she looked comfortable. I poured her a glass of wine as she pulled up a stool to the island.

"No, I don't mind at all. You look rather warm, cute, and comfortable. I figured I would have me a little something to drink before I turn in for the night. I also figured it would be rude not to pour you a glass as well. It's wine. I hope it's not a bit much and you don't think too far into it or anything. I don't want you to think that I am trying to get you drunk and take advantage of you. When I am alone I generally go in the study and sip something a little stronger."

"Wine is fine, Kyle. No, I didn't think you meant anything by it. You don't come off as the type to take advantage of someone," she replied, laughing as she lifted the glass to her lips.

"Well, I'm glad that you are well aware of that. How's Chelsie settling in with her aunt living in town opposed to being far away?" I asked.

"I think she likes it just fine. We have been spending a lot of time together. I don't consume all of her time or smother her. I give her space being that she is a teenager with friends and all. I don't want her to feel bombarded or obligated just because I moved closer. Although, she is the main reason I moved back in town. There might be a slight chance I would get a teaching spot at her high school." I could tell Kira was excited about the whole ordeal. She rambled on about it with no clue of hidden agenda or plot in her voice or demeanor. I wanted to jump right out and ask her but I figured I should let her do the opening up. Forcing her might cause a ripple in her plans. I wouldn't want to ruin anything for her or Chelsie if all that I have heard was true. Plus, I couldn't come up with any clever way to get her to just come right out with it or lead up into such a conversation that could also possibly ruin our time together tonight.

"How are your parents handling the relief of an extra helping hand?" I still hadn't met her folks yet neither. I wasn't all that anxious to meet her father in the first place, being that he has no reputation of being a people person in the community. It is something that just has to be done, being that I value family. Besides, I don't think there is anyone left to meet on my side except for Mr. Robinson.

"Mother and I have always been close even though we didn't get all the mother daughter time together like others raising their daughter. I can tell she likes me in town a little more. We go out to lunch, grocery shop, and work on small projects around the house together. My father and I really haven't had that much of a relationship. We have our little talks from time to time and that is about it. I would say that I am a more of a mother's daughter than a daddy's girl. He takes real good care of Chelsie, though. I guess he focused all of his fatherly duties on her being that she lost her parents. I just kind of took the backseat. Chelsie loves her papaw as well." The whole time we were talking, she never showed any signs that there could be anything more to what we were discussing.

"Technically, you have met all of my family except for Mr. Robinson. Do you think I will ever bump into your family some day?" I asked this question as lightly as I could by adding a little humor to it. She responded as though she never heard me or caught it.

"Kyle, how is your life now? I mean, do you somewhat wish to know who your parents are? What if they showed up at your door or at work today? How would you respond? Would you accept them? Would you try to have some sort of relationship with them? Would you rejoice or reject the moment?" Here I was digging and she flipped it on me with this question. Once again, she was trying to find a way to evade the issue.

It took a minute as I was absorbing the question and thought of what if my parents showed up one day. How would I truly act if my parents showed up out of the blue? I took a sip and finally answered. "I'm not sure how I would respond. Part of me would be angry maybe and part of me would be somewhat eased to put names and faces together. I really don't hold any grudges as far as how I ended up. I truly ended up with one of, if not the best family in town. I had wonderful caretakers who I grew up calling mom and dad. Truly my life isn't that bad. I guess my issue with them is just simply being thrown away. If they didn't want me then, why would they come looking for me now? Like you said at the nursing home, they didn't even try to keep somewhat of a close eye on me. I would never abandon my child. That alone leaves me to wonder why. I think that would be the topic of our reunion if they did show up out of the blue. What were your reasons? What were you thinking by leaving me in a suit case on the doorstep of the nursing home?" The more I talked about it; I could sense myself getting a little frustrated at the thought. Part of me would want that missing piece of the puzzle to take its final place.

"Do you think you are better off not knowing and things being the way they are, or do you want to know? Do you think it would make your life easier or harder?" Kira was really digging with this topic. Why so concerned about me and my abandonment all of a sudden? I don't even think I look like it bothers me. As a matter of fact, I don't even bring it up or talk about it. Where was all of this coming from? Why should I answer all of her questions and she always evade mine. I could feel myself getting a little frustrated about the matter. So I pulled one of her stunts.

"I can't really give you an answer on how it would make my life pertaining to harder or easier. My life is pretty simple now with one piece missing. I guess you could say that it may complicate my life for a while. Who is to say how I would react? Right now I wouldn't receive them with open arms and act like everything was peachy. I would want my questions answered. Then maybe, depending on their reasons, things might change." I had gotten to the point to where I didn't want to talk about it anymore. The more we discussed it, the more uncomfortable I was getting. I didn't want to misuse the time she and I have together. So I changed the subject by ending the night as we were already sipping the last of our glasses. "Baby, it is getting awfully late. I don't want to keep you up and I do have to work in the morning. I think I am headed to bed. Either room you chose to sleep in will be fine with me."

"Well, what room do you sleep in, Kyle?" Kira asked as she was finishing her last sip and I was rinsing out my glass.

That was another question I wasn't expecting tonight but way more comfortable to talk about than the last. "I really like, you Kira. I know we have been drinking and…"

"Sleep, Kyle, just like you, all I want is to sleep. I'm not expecting anything or trying to seduce you." Kira interrupted me while laughing.

"I sleep in the master bedroom," answering with a smile on my face. I admit I was getting a little nervous. I turned off the light in the kitchen and she followed me up the stairs to the bed room. My goodness, she was truly beautiful. I honestly hope nothing happens tonight. I hope I can contain myself. Outside all that I have heard and feel I need to find out, she is still special to me. I just think it is too soon to be doing anything extreme right now. Once we got under the covers, her body began to make its way to mine. As her back made contact with my chest, she reached back and pulled my arm around her.

"Good night, Kyle," she said, exhaling while her body sunk into to mine.

"Sweet dreams, dear." There was that wonderful smell of her hair again. My pulse was racing while it seemed like my heart was about to beat its way out of my chest.

Slowly I began to calm down. We laid there in utter silence for a moment, and she and I both were off to sleep.

I had awoken to the sun peeking through the window into my face. I was alone in my bed. Kira must have woken up before I did. I rose to my feet looking over at the clock on the dresser. My alarm was to go off in five minutes. I called out for Kira, but there was no answer. I got up and headed down stairs to check and see if she was down there already. I could smell food as I made my way toward the kitchen. Breakfast was on the island; next to the plate was a note.

"Good morning, sweetheart. You looked so peaceful, I couldn't wake you up. I hope you enjoy your breakfast as much as I enjoy time with you. Hope you have a great day and find time to think of me here and there. Miss me, Kira."

I smiled as I finished the note. Breakfast was a simple bacon, eggs, and toast, but taste better than any other with the thought of Kira on my mind. She seems to be an amazing woman. I love everything about her and adore her beauty. Hopefully everything works itself out smoothly. After breakfast, I showered, got dressed, and headed to work.

The day started out like any other day. After I entered the building, I stopped at the front desk to get my folder from Mrs. Sharon.

"Hello, dear!" I said while thumbing through the paperwork in the folder.

"Why, good morning, Mr. McCormic, in good spirits today I see. What has our activities director in such a good mood this morning? Must be a woman! It wouldn't be that little ole gal that returned that blanket here at the front desk that day, would it?" I could tell she was teasing me with all the sarcasm in her voice, but she was absolutely right. Kira has made things a little easier for me. It's nice to have someone special for once.

"Yes, ma'am. Her name is Kira. She and I are still together so far. She is really a great person. I enjoy spending time with her," I replied happily with confidence.

"Well, that is good. I overheard your mother talking about her with one of the residents out in the garden. I could tell Mrs. Brenda really likes her as well by the way she was going on and on." The word amongst the staff must be spreading fast with Mrs. Sharon knowing. She always has the latest scoops and inquiries on all the staff here at the Nursing Home. She never claims to be nosey. She says a little "ear hustle" is not really called being nosey. I'd say it's nosey, but she brought good news today. So I will let her off the hook. We finished our conversation and I then headed to mother's quarters before going to my office and getting my day started.

Once I arrived, I knocked on the door as I entered her domain. The television was down low, she and Mr. Robinson were in the living room having tea and coffee. I think Mr. Robinson had been stopping by as much as I have for the last year or so. He and the McCormic family have always been close but his stops have begun to be more frequent. I'm sure there is nothing to it. Besides, they are my family and I enjoy seeing them both.

"Hello, son! Your mother and I were just talking about you this morning. She was telling me about Kira. You and Kira are getting more and more serious? I assume things are well between the two of you?" Mother and Mr. Robinson both were smiling from ear to ear as he was questioning me about Kira.

"Yes, sir. She is a really nice girl. She and I have been spending quite some time together," I replied with a smile, rubbing the back of my neck, eyes to the floor as though I may have been a little bashful about it.

"How do Mr. and Mrs. Alexander feel about you two?" Instantly the smile was wiped off my face. I still hadn't met her parents and I don't know if she has said anything to them about me. Mr. Robinson had opened a can of worms with that question.

I replied anyway. "I haven't met her parents yet, sir. I honestly can't tell you if she has even told them. Besides that, everything is going great. She has spent a few nights here and there at the house. Nothing has happened mother, I was a complete gentleman," quickly grabbing my mother's hand to ease her thoughts of her son, as I replied to Mr. Robinson. She laughed at the comment and shook her head.

"Have you asked to meet her parents? Perhaps schedule a lunch of some sort with her and her folks? I'm sure once they meet you and get to know you, things will be fine. Maybe even ease your mind a little bit. Heck, maybe I should schedule a lunch with the two of you, being that I am the only one of your family she hasn't met yet." Laughing as he spoke. He seemed highly interested in meeting her. Mr. Robinson is a very important person in my life. It would be nice for her to meet him and him to meet my first potential mate. The more I thought about it, the more important it was becoming.

"Sir, that wouldn't be a bad idea. Maybe we all can hang out at the house, me, you, mom, and Kira?"

Mother chimed in. "That sounds like a good idea son. I think that would really be nice. Besides, I think I have a few things at the house that I may be looking for. That would also give me the opportunity to retrieve them. Plus, I was thinking that I could spend the weekend there also. Surely we could work something out son?"

"The nursing home has never had a problem with me taking you home and you spending more than a day away. I'm sure it won't take much. A weekend with my favorite people does sound nice. Kira and I are planning to leave for a weekend in the mountains with the gang for a small get away or mini vacation. I am kind of looking forward to it, to be honest." I felt more comfortable than I did when I was trying to piece things together out of the situation that remains a mystery.

"Well, that does sound great. A small vacation away from the everyday hustle and bustle might be just what I need as well. If not a vacation, how about you and I go catch a ball game together? It has been a while since you and I have spent some quality time together. I really enjoy the time you and I spend together. Always have, since you were a baby boy. You are more than like family to me, like a son I would say." It has been a while since Mr. Robinson and I had our day planned. We have always done things together. He was right about the family part and he has always treated me like a son.

"You're right, Mr. Robinson. I'm sure we can find a game to attend. I think I could use a little travel and chitchat with my go-to guy. I believe we should take off during this week before this weekend."

Mother spoke immediately after I finished my sentence. "You boys should spend some time together. I think that would be great and much needed also. Taking time off this week may cut into our scheduled visits but I have been wanting some time to myself for my special project. I am little behind and I do want to get this done." You could tell by Mother's voice that she was all for it.

"What's the rush, Mother? What project are you working on now?" She usually involves me in all her projects but I don't think she ever mentioned any new one to me.

"I'm just in a hurry to get things done son. I'm getting older and slower. This project is my own personal project. I have been working on it for years I guess you could say. I believe I'm nearly finished. It is my best one yet. Hopefully everyone will like it when it's finished. I have truly put my heart into this one. Kenneth never knew about it. I didn't expect him to leave so soon. I was hoping everyone would be around for its finishing touches." I never have seen mother work on anything consistently over the years. While she was talking, I was replaying everything I have seen her do over the years to see if I could catch a hint for a good guess. All the ones I remembered, I was involved in until its completion. I had nothing to stand on for this mysterious project and I wasn't going to pressure mother into telling me. She said it was better than all the others and her heart was into it. I wouldn't want to cause her any trouble with badgering her to tell me.

We had been chatting for a while now. If Mr. Robinson and I were going to take a day off this week, then I needed to get some things done. "I reckon I should hurry along now. If we are to take off this week, I better have some things finished early sir," I said as I looked at my watch then everyone else in the room.

"Me too, son, I have a small projects list that I should get started on and close to completion if I am going to miss a day also. I guess we both should be going." I kissed and hugged my mother goodbye. Mr. Robinson followed out the door behind me after hugging Mother goodbye as well.

Once we got to my office, I turned and faced Mr. Robinson as he was coming down the hallway behind me. "I guess we will catch a game in a couple of days, sir?" I asked with a smile as I placed my hand on his shoulder.

"A couple of days sound about right, son. I will be ready," he replied with a smile and glare in his eyes. Noticing this smile and glare, the response stuck with me as he was walking away. I paused in my doorway for a minute as I watched him make his way to his office. I never gave anything as much thought as the smile, the glare, and the squeeze of his hand on my shoulder. Surely nothing was wrong I hope. Mr. Robinson was never good at keeping secrets. I'm sure I would at least be the first or second to hear the news. If there is something wrong, surely he will talk about it on our trip together this week. As he disappeared around the corner, I turned and went into my office.

I had gotten an extra days work done for the day like I had planned. Mr. Robinson was still on my mind. As I was leaving the office, I stopped by his maintenance office, but he was nowhere to be found. I assumed he had some project he may have been working on here at the facility. I said my goodbyes for the day and left to head home. As I was driving home, I began to reflect on the events of today and all that was going on around me, thinking that I have a good relationship with a great girl and a great family. It's just that now, everybody seemed so secretive. Finding out about Kira's situation is still out in the open. Now it's also mother, and Mr. Robinson adding to the mysteries. I know it may not be anything to worry about, but I couldn't help but to wonder, what project could mother have been working on over the years? Her projects weren't really projects. They were her special way for us to spend time together as mother and son. You can't help but to tell something is heavily on Mr. Robinsons mind with the way he acted today. I mean maybe he has told mother. Maybe I should talk to mother and ask her if there is anything concerning Mr. Robinson that I may be able to help with. They do spend quite a lot of time together. The more I thought, the more concerned I had gotten. They did show up at the house a few days ago unexpected. That hasn't happened in years. Maybe they are just trying to spend a lot of quality time now that they are getting older. Then again, Mr. Robinson isn't that much older than me, maybe about nineteen or twenty years. I would say mother maybe had twenty-five or thirty years on Mr. Robinson. I guess I should try to worry less for now and just give them both the benefit of the doubt. Worrying about everyone around you could be too much to bear, especially if things turn out not to be all that serious to worry about.

Once I arrived at the house, I stopped by the study and placed the needle on the record as I headed up stairs to take a shower. After I finished getting cleaned up, I came back to the study, poured myself a drink, sat down, and began to look for a game or event we may be able to attend this week. Selections were few but I did find a college basketball game online. It was the college that Mr. Robinson had played for before his knee injury. I thought this could be a great idea. Being in his old alma mater atmosphere may lift his spirits, give him some good memories and stories to tell me while we are there. I immediately bought seats as close to the court as I could get us. I think I will surprise Mr. Robinson with the news tomorrow at work. I sure hope that he will like the idea of going back to his old college. He would always reflect back on his old college ball days. Mr. Robinson was loaded with stories and how he played against some of the guys that were in the pros. Mom and Dad believed Mr. Robinson was as good as any in basketball and could have very well been a professional basketball player like the rest.

I felt myself starting to doze off as I finished my second drink, so I took my last sip, and headed to bed.

I woke up the next morning to the alarm blaring on the night stand on the side of the bed. I thought to myself, "Now surely I didn't have that much to drink." I must have been really sleeping good to not want to wake up to the sound of the alarm. I started my day off in my usual routine, out of bed and straight into the shower. Once I had gotten done and dressed, I made my way down the stairs and into the kitchen. I could hear the record still playing in the study. I must have been so tired last night that I had forgotten to take the needle off the record before leaving the study. After turning off the record, I made my way to the kitchen for breakfast. As I was eating breakfast, I thought more and more about our plans. We should stay all night and maybe have a night out after the game. Maybe go to a nice restaurant or something, somewhere where he and I could have some time to talk man to man. On my way to work I called Kira to see if she would like to go out to dinner tonight after work. She told me that she didn't have anything planned for the day and that it would be a date. My true intentions tonight are to bring up meeting her parents. Personally, I had too many mysteries in my head and wanted to start getting some answers. If the story about her and her family is true, I was ready to find out and move on the next step. Whether it keeps us together or divides us, I was ready for the suspense to be over. I had already had my mind made up. I really liked Kira. I was prepared to try and support her in any way I could. Things are great between the both of us. It just seems unfair for her to go at things alone if the story is true.

The nursing home seemed kind of dry this morning as I made it in to the front desk. I didn't have much to do, so I headed to my mother's living quarters before going into my office.

"Knock, knock," I said as I entered my mother's domain. I could smell oatmeal cooking and coffee brewing. "Sure smells delicious in here," I said out load as I entered the kitchen. Mother and Mrs. Sharon were standing next to the stove.

"Good morning, Mr. McCormic."

"Good morning, Mrs. Sharon, Mother," I greeted Mrs. Sharon as I hugged mother. Mrs. Sharon knew who my mother was but rarely did I see them together. Mrs. Sharon was much younger than mother. I think she may have worked a year or two with mother when she first started and mother was getting ready to retire. This was kind of a surprise to me, so I waited for Mrs. Sharon to leave, before asking mother what was the matter of her morning visitor.

"She was stopping by to talk about Mr. Robinson. She said he called in today. She said that he had called and said that he wasn't feeling well. I told her he may not be feeling well. She said he didn't sound too good. She did seem highly concerned, but he hasn't really told me anything about his health. Has he said anything to you dear? As Mother was telling me about Mrs. Sharon's show of concern and Mr. Robinson calling in, I couldn't help not to think about how he acted yesterday. He did seem like something was heavily on his mind.

As I was leaving mother to get started on my day, I dialed Mr. Robinson's home phone number but I didn't get an answer. I figured he may have been out, busy, or wanted some alone time if something may have been going on with him. Surely Mother would have been the first person to know if something was up. I could understand hiding it from Mrs. Sharon, but hopefully not me. I will call and check on him later before I meet up with Kira. I hope nothing is wrong, nor will we have to cancel our plans together. The game is two days away from now. I hope he will be up to par by then. Being that I was going to ask Kira about her family today and now Mr. Robinson just topped my worries, things were beginning to pile up.

Before leaving the nursing home, I stopped by the front desk for a second. I wanted to check with Mrs. Sharon again on how Mr. Robinson might have seemed over the phone. She said that she could tell that he wasn't feeling all that well, but he didn't say what was going on with him. He just called and notified her that he would not be in today. She asked me if I had any knowledge of anything that might be going on with him. Of course I was as clueless as she was and mother didn't think anything could be wrong with him. Surely things will come to light here in the next few days.

I didn't stay long because Kira was to meet me at the house before we went out to eat. Outside of everything else, a nice dinner with my special girl didn't sound like a bad idea. Of course, I was going to ask her about meeting her family which may cause some more problems. Kira didn't show up long after I had gotten home and cleaned up. I had left the door unlocked before I got in the shower. She was sitting in the kitchen at the island having a glass of wine as I came down the stairs after getting dressed.

"Is everything all right?" I know this was a date, but I didn't expect to do any drinking tonight. When I saw the glass of wine, I immediately thought something was wrong or maybe she had a long day.

"No, dear, everything is all right now that I am here with my favorite man in the whole world. How was your day?" she replied as she downed the last of her glass, getting up, wrapping her arms around my neck, and greeting me with a kiss. "So what is on our agenda for the night? Seems like we haven't been around each other in forever. I really have been missing you lately. I got excited when you called for dinner." She was very high spirited tonight. She seemed so into us, but then again, it may have been her buzzing from the wine.

"I figured we could go somewhere nice and romantic. Later take a walk or something," I answered while staring into her beautiful eyes. I truly was happy to be with her. She never failed at making me feel wanted and special. With my issue of being abandoned and her issue of being an outcast, I felt like we had something spiritually in common. I know that may be a strange way of putting it but it was the best way I could describe it.

Dinner went well. We had spent most of the time laughing and catching up on our brief time apart from each other. We even had a little reflection back to the first time we met at the game. She said that she had always gone to her niece's school events, but never really met anyone or engaged in much conversation. I could tell in her conversation that she had always gone alone. It was intriguing that her parents never attended these events with her. Instead of going out for a walk, we ended back home on the couch in front of the fire place in the living room. It was quiet for a moment. I didn't want to ruin the night but I finally mustard up the courage to dig in, I had to ask.

"So every time that you came in town for Chelsie, your parents never attended any of her events with you?" I was nervous. It had gotten a little quieter after asking the question.

"No, my father and I don't get along well. Mother and I do communicate and also spend a little time together but she wasn't in to all those things. They love Chelsie, don't get me wrong. They just distance themselves while I'm in town with her. My father and I haven't seen eye to eye in years. I know my mother loves me. She just does her best to keep the peace. I can understand things from her perspective. She has to live with my father while trying to not completely cast me out. Even Chelsie is starting to take notice and ask me questions from time to time." Kira had never really gone into depth about the division in her family. This was my first time hearing it from her. I think she may have had too much to drink and forgotten that I wasn't aware of such division.

"Why do you think you guys are so divided? Is it because you and your sister were sent off to private school?" I could tell she was getting upset and uncomfortable with the questioning. She slid off of the couch and proceeded into the kitchen. We ended up in the kitchen and she started to pour another glass of wine.

"I think it was after the shipwreck really. Losing a child can be devastating. Maybe he never recovered from it and casting me out in fear of losing me could be his way of handling the issue. I know it's not the right way to handle things but that may be it helps him in some sort of way, I don't know." She wouldn't make eye contact with me. She just drank and stared off into the glass, massaging its neck of the wine glass as she was talking.

"How were you and your sister with your father before the accident that happened out at sea?" I was aware of how uncomfortable she was, but I just kept on digging with the questions. "Do you think that I will ever meet your parents? How will they feel about us or me in general that I am not of the same race?

Kira closed her eyes and withdrew the glass from her lips. "Why are you so concerned with my relationship with my parents or my family, Kyle? What does it matter to you if you meet them or if you're black? Why is all this suddenly so flipping important to you?" She was beginning to raise her voice in frustration. I didn't want to fight, nor did I know how to answer the question without coming right out with all that I have heard the past few weeks. I didn't respond at all. Slowly reached over, gently pulled her off the stool into my arms. Tears had formed and started traveling down her face as she was in my arms.

"Kyle, I'm sorry. It's time for me to leave." She broke my arms free from around her and headed for the door. I asked for her to wait and come back as she slammed the front door exiting the house. I stood there in silence as I heard the ignition and squealing of tires as she left. As I cleaned up the kitchen, I started to wonder if I had made a foul move by getting her to talk about her family. Had I pushed her away instead of trying to get her to open up? Could this be the end of us? Maybe she won't talk to me anymore after tonight. After I straightened up everything, I went to the study to think. Drinking heavily while replaying all that just happened, I called Kira to apologize, but I only got her voicemail. I hope she made it home safely at least. I had called several times before dozing off at my desk in the study. She had turned her phone off of by the seventh call.

The next morning, I had found myself waking up in the study. My head was pounding as I could barely hear the alarm in my room blaring. I must have had too much to drink last night. I immediately took something for my head, went upstairs to silence the alarm. I realized that I was two hours late for work as I was reaching for the clock to turn off the alarm on the night stand in my bedroom. I took a quick shower and darted out the door to work. On the way, I called Kira two more times after checking my phone to see that she had not returned my calls. I was truly worried that I had made things worse and ruined our relationship. Maybe it was bad timing or the wrong approach, but I was only trying to help. Hopefully she will realize that my intentions were good, and maybe give us a chance to talk this out.

I entered in through a side door closer to mother's quarters when I arrived at work. I was already late, plus in a hurry to talk to mom. When I had gotten to her room, she and Mr. Robinson were sitting at the table having breakfast. Both had smiles on their faces, so I assumed he was better and everything was all right.

"Good morning, son. I had told your mother that I had stopped by your office before coming down here. I noticed you weren't there or in your usual areas. Are you running late this morning?" he said sarcastically as he acknowledged me entering the room.

"Long night last night, sir, rough night," I replied while shaking my head. "Hey, pretty lady, how are you this morning?" I said as I hugged Mother, kissing her on the cheek.

"Fine, dear. John and I were just talking about the old days while eating a little breakfast. There is some left in the kitchen if you would like to join us. It's not a whole lot, I didn't know if you would be coming after John told me he didn't see any sign of you this morning." I sat down to join them after gathering what was left to eat in the kitchen.

"Oh, I found something for us to do in a couple of days, sir. How would you like to go watch a ball game at your old college up north?" When I bought those tickets, I envisioned a better response than the one Mr. Robinson gave.

"You bought tickets to my old college? I guess that could be fun," he replied looking at mother the whole time he was responding to my idea of going to the game. His look of surprise was different than the one I expected he would have. I didn't bother asking what was wrong with the idea being that I had already caused chaos between Kira and me last night. I just simply ignored his demeanor and kept talking and eating.

"How is your relationship with Kira going, dear?" Mother asked.

"Okay, I reckon. I may have overstepped my boundary last night, though."

"How so, what happened?" Mother could tell it was serious by how dry I sounded answering her question.

"We went out to dinner last night, ended up back at this house for a few drinks while sitting in front of the fire place in the living room. We got on the subject of her and her family. I asked a few questions on meeting Chelsie and possibly her parents. The more questions I asked, the more emotionally, irritated, and irate she got. To make a long story short, she ended up storming out of the house in tears. I tried calling her from then up until now and so far I've not received one returned phone call."

"Oh, dear, I'm sorry. How do you feel about what happened?"

"I mean. It needed to happen. I feel bad about her feelings, but if we are to move forward, we need to be open. It needed to happen. Now whether she calls back, we talk it out, or break up is on her. I hate how things ended up, but deep down, I just don't feel like it was a bad move." Though I felt bad about her feelings, it had to be done. I didn't intend to hurt her feelings. I was trying to show her that I was in her corner no matter what.

"She will come around, son. Just give her some time. I imagine it is hard for her to open up after living like however for so many years. Just give it some time." Mr. Robinson chimed in, adding light to the matter but leaving me in darkness about the other. My question is when will he come around? Something seems off about everyone around me. I thought it may have been me at first but everyone is acting so strange. I'm sure I will light Mr. Robinson's fire in a couple of days. Then somewhere down the line ruffle my mother's feathers. Because there must be something between the two of them by the blank stare she returned to Mr. Robinson while giving a response on attending the game.

CHAPTER EIGHT

"He's with me." I told the lady at the entrance, as I showed her our tickets, making our way into the game. As we were entering the gym, I couldn't help but to keep my attention on Mr. Robinson's demeanor. His attention was everywhere as he followed behind me while making our way to our seats. We had court side seats across from the home team's bench.

"Everything okay, sir?" I asked as I was referring to the seating and view.

"Yes, yes, everything is nice. You did good, son. It's been a while since I have been here. A lot has changed, hard to get that 'right at home' feeling but everything is perfect," Mr. Robinson responded as he was still looking all around, removing his jacket.

"I know it has been a while, sir. You don't see any familiar faces anywhere, do you?"

"Naw, naw, can't say that I have. Heck, that was the main reason I had been doing all this looking around," he replied with a quick laugh. "Oh well. Let's go, Knights!" he yelled as he finally turned his attention to the game. Maybe I am overreacting. I thought to myself as I began to join him in routing on the home team.

As the game went on, Mr. Robinson had gotten more relaxed. He told me how things had changed since he attended school here. How the floor had changed, the entrance, and how the school added the trophy case in the concession area. He told me that he had come home his junior year and never came back to finish. He earned his degree at the local technical college back home. He told me how maintenance was all he and my father had down around the house and with the rental properties. So he felt like maintenance was the only thing he knew other than basketball.

After the game ended, we made our way to the trophy case by the concession stand. The photos and trophies were arranged by the year of the season.

"Mr. Robinson, what year were you here, sir?"

"About five years down, Kyle," he responded while glaring off into the trophy case.

"John, John Robinson?" A not-so-sure voice caught our attention as we arrived at the years of Mr. Robinson's attendance. Mr. Robinson wasn't too sure who the man was before he introduced himself. "John, it's me, Will, Will Stallons, Stally."

"Stally! How are you doing, brother? My, it's been a while. I saw you in the pros for a couple seasons. I wondered what had happened to you." Mr. Robinson seemed more excited once the strange man had introduced himself and he remembered who he was.

"Man, not too bad. I'm the head coach here now. I thought that was you I had seen across the floor. It sure has been a long time. It sure is good to see you. Everyone lost touch with you after you left school. Is this your son? Boy, your father was one of the greatest players to pick up a basketball. I played in the pros and I believe to this day that he could have been one of the greats." I finally corrected the man as he was ranting on and on about Mr. Robinson.

"No, sir. He is a good friend of the family and we work together now. He is like a father to me though. I've known John all of my life."

"Kyle, why don't you give me and Coach Stally a few minutes? Wait here at the trophy case for me?" Mr. Robinson interrupted me as I was correcting Coach Stally. As they walked a distance away, I returned to admiring the years of Mr. Robinson's attendance. What coach Stally was saying must have been true. I noticed how much of the case Mr. Robinson had taken up. The school had won two conference titles in his attendance. The case was loaded with newspaper clippings of Mr. Robinson. He was the player of the year twice. He holds second place in the schools scoring record, next to William Stallons, Coach Stally. I noticed that Coach Stallons broke his record in his fourth year. A few pictures had caught my attention though.

There was a section where the men's and women's basketball team won titles in their conference the same year. It was in Mr. Robinson's last year. There I saw pictures of the women's team along with the men's team. There were a few photos of the women practicing with the men and what seemed like a big men vs. women's event by the crowd in the back ground. The pictures gained more of my interest as I saw photos of the game where the camera was focused on one on one shots of the woman that Mr. Robinson was guarding during the game. These photos plus the championship ceremony photo of just her and him stuck out in my mind. These photos represented more than just a great season to me. The camera was capturing more than just two athletes for the same school. Her name was Jo Anna Kilo. I got her name from the women's team photo.

"Hey, son, ready to roll out? How about we find us a bite to eat somewhere? Maybe grab some sodas afterward?" Mr. Robinson suggested silently walking up behind me catching me by surprise. I couldn't help but to think that he may have been standing behind me for a minute while I was trying to figure out that one particular section of the trophy case.

After leaving the college, we found a sports bar about a mile and a half down the road. As we sat there eating and drinking our sodas, all I could think about was Jo Anna Kilo. It seems like she was a good basketball player, but other things stuck out in my mind besides basketball. She was an extremely beautiful woman. Whether there was more to the photos is questionable, friends or lovers? The more I thought, the more I wondered, and the deeper the pit in my stomach had gotten.

"What's the matter, son? You seem like you have changed since the game. Is something bothering you?" Mr. Robinson had totally interrupted my thoughts. I had been so deep in thought that I imagine I hadn't spoken to him since the trophy case.

"Who was Jo Anna Kilo?" With no wonder, no hesitation, no second thought the question shot out of my mouth like a rocket from a bazooka.

Mr. Robinson slowly put down his glass. "Jo Anna Kilo. Jo Anna was the women's star basketball player at the time that I was attending school and playing for the basketball team. One of the best females I have ever seen pick up a basketball. She loved sports, and was extremely competitive. She was a year ahead of me but we had become good friends in the years that I attended. She knew she was a good ball player but felt the only way the girls to team could be effective was to practice against the men. She felt the only way for her to get better was to match up against me every day. We became such good friends. All she could talk about was sports. Other than that, I don't think she could hold any other conversation." Mr. Robinson stared off into space as he went on and on about this Jo Anna Kilo.

Suddenly stopping him in mid conversation, "but you two were more than friends weren't you?" I asked with a deep stare into his eyes. In the minute of silence before he answered, I couldn't remember one time I had even seen Mr. Robinson date or even hear the name Jo Anna Kilo from his mouth.

"Very much so, Kyle, very much so. I lost more than my career after leaving college. After the injury, I tried to play again, but I had re-injured the same knee. Not being able to play again was depressing and effecting my school work and attendance. I knew I would soon return home. She loved basketball so much that she couldn't give up her dreams of becoming a star. So the option of her moving back home with me was out. Outside of sports, what little time she had for me was fading. So instead of sticking around, we said our goodbyes. Mr. and Mrs. McCormic was all I had left. For years they had helped me through the depression. I went through so much in so little time. Life truly seemed over for me with no basketball and especially no Jo Anna." It pained him to answer my question. Deep down, I was feeling guilty for bringing up old feelings and ruining Mr. Robinson's night.

"I'm sorry, sir. I didn't mean to bring about any old pains or bad memories."

"No, not at all, son, don't feel guilty. You did nothing wrong. I'm over it now. I still had a good life, with a great family. The McComics have been so good to me. I never had the chance of being a father but you are more than a friend to me in more ways than I can explain or you will ever know. As crazy as it sounds, I still keep a part of her around. Listening to records and playing chess seemed to be an unbreakable habit. I would say a piece of her had always stuck with me. She hated losing." He smiled as he replied.

"Do you have any idea of what ever happened to her?"

"After leaving school, we lost touch. The last I had ever heard of her, she had moved overseas to play women's basketball. I imagine she is retired now and probably still over there somewhere." Even though he answered all my questions, I still had a strong curiosity about Ms. Kilo. Part of me wanted to find her for Mr. Robinson but why and what good would it do if she wouldn't have anything to do with him anymore. I hate that he lost his love. Like I said, it must have been damaging because I have no memory of him ever dating again.

After the conversation, I paid for our drinks and food, then, we headed to the hotel. Little was said the rest of the night. He mainly talked about his three year career at school and the friendship between him and coach Stally. He shared a lot of memories with me minus talking about Jo Anna. It may be a thing of the past with him but part of me just can't let it go. If a relationship is good, then why let it go? Mr. Robinson has always been encouraging and supportive of me. He has never seemed like the type to hold anyone back from being successful or achieving their goals. If they would have stayed together, there would have been a strong possibility that I would have never met Mr. Robinson. I would have never known him or had him in my life, but knowing the man that I know today, he would have been happy. That's what counts the most, not that I could say he isn't happy with his life now. Why would she turn away a great guy like Mr. Robinson?

After getting back into town, I called Kira and still received no answer. I was truly worried if I should give her time or just expect to never see her again. I unpacked, cleaned up at the house a little bit then called Jacs for lunch. I was truly overwhelmed and needed someone outside of all the mischief to talk to, like a neutral party.

Jacs met me at Alice's Café for lunch. She had made it there before I did. She had reserved my favorite table. The one I sat at and showed to Kira the night we met.

"So what's the big bother, Kyle?"

As soon as she asked, I felt like all things had jumbled up at once and I didn't know which issue to address first. After pausing for a moment, I just spit out the first thing that came to mind. "I don't know about Kira. We had a talk the other night after dinner that didn't end so well. I haven't heard from her since then."

"Wow, that bad, huh, what did you two talk about?"

I had forgotten how long it has been since we all hung out and talked. Jacs nor the fellas were up to speed on what was going on in my life or with Kira and me. "I asked her if I would ever meet her parents and her niece. She acted as though if none of that was important, then proceeded to get angry as I kept on discussing the subject. She finally had enough and stormed out the door. I've called every day since then but I have received no answer nor returned call. After this long, I think there might be a chance that things are over between us. I had no intentions of making things complicated. I was only trying to help and be there for her. Now, I feel like I have made a mess of things and made her life a little more difficult."

"Difficult? Wait a minute, Kyle, have I missed something? Trying to help? I'm a bit lost here. I know it has been a month after the wedding, but what has happened? What is going on? Bring me up to speed." I was talking to Jacs like she had known what was going on. She had no clue on what I was talking about.

"Kira's story about her family, her niece, her sister, and her history in this town doesn't add up or make sense. No one knows her. Everybody seems to know little about her parents and family background. All the people I have talked to don't seem to remember the Alexanders having two children. Everybody says they had one daughter. Kira only talks about her sister when I ask. She rarely talks about her father or mother. She keeps the conversations about her niece to a minimum. I have been doing some research around town, but only with the people I know and that are close to me. I have a gut feeling that things aren't what she says they are and that her niece may be her daughter. When I said I was only trying to help, I meant be her support if she was trying to change things with her family. I have a strong feeling that something isn't right."

"Wow, I knew we didn't know much about her but all these possibilities you are telling me about, I had never thought of. That is a story you just don't here every day."

She seemed so surprised and devastated.

"Really, Jacs, what about me, look at my life? I have no idea who my parents are. I've been raised by white people all my life. I'm a black man with white parents. Kira's story is no more strange or puzzling than this you see every day." I began to get frustrated with myself as I was going on about my life. I had Mr. Robinson and JoAnna Kilo in the back of my mind as I was ranting and raving.

"Whoa now, Kyle, hold up. We have discussed this already and there is no need to head down this road again. You know I, we all love you. Whether you find out who's your real parents or not, love the ones who loved you. As for Kira, give her time. Whether it is over with or on hold. Just give her some time. I'm sure once she has cooled off and gathered herself, she will let you know what to do." Jacs was right. She really put me in my place. All of these issues at once are weighing on me.

"I just feel overwhelmed and defenseless with all that is going on. I'm sorry, Jacs. Thanks for listening and the feedback. I really needed to vent and get things off my chest." After I apologized, Jacs soon changed the subject. She started to tell me about her first month of marriage between her and Marcus. She had my stomach in knots from laughing so hard about his habits and the small lifestyle changes they were going through as husband and wife. We soon finished our dinner and headed our separate ways. Before we left, she did remind me about our trip up north to the cabins.

On my way home, I changed from worrying about Kira to Mr. Robinson and Jo Anna Kilo. In my heart, I felt there was more than what Mr. Robinson was telling me. How could someone give up such a great guy? His story made her seem so selfish? The fact that he was unable to play basketball anymore, made her withdraw her love for him? I truly had to get in touch with mother about this issue. I even felt that I needed to make a trip to see Coach Stally. I'm sure there was a reason for Mr. Robinson excusing the two of them from my presence.

When I turned into the driveway to the house, I noticed Kira's car was parked in the driveway. As I had gotten closer, I noticed Kira sitting on the porch, arms folded across her knees, and head tucked down in her arms. I couldn't see her face until I approached her, "Kira?"

She slowly lifted her head. She had tears streaming down her face. I immediately lifted her up and escorted her in the house. As I was asking her what's the matter I fixed her glass of water. Before I could hand it to her, she had taken off to the living room to sit down.

As I handed her the water and a cloth for her tears, she spoke and said, "I'm sorry, Kyle. I'm sorry for going off on you and storming out. I know you are trying to help me, but there is something you need to know and understand first. I haven't completely been honest with you about who I am. I have never gotten this close to anyone in my life since I was young. Everything was going so well between us. I figured I could solve everything and tell you later. The other night just made me feel so guilty and uncomfortable. Guilty for not being completely honest and upfront with you, and, at the moment, I felt if I had told you, then you would push me away. You would think terrible of me." She came across the couch, threw her head in my chest, and went back to crying heavily.

"Wait, what are you hiding and so scared to tell me? What could be so bad that would turn me away from you or ruin things between us?" I gently pulled her away from my chest and wiped her tears. I played as if didn't have a general idea of what she was about to tell me. I knew that the real story was getting ready to unfold right now at this moment. I after all the digging and the research, I was getting ready to hear the real story from the source itself.

"I don't know how or any other way to tell you other than how exactly things happened to get my life where it is now. My life is so screwed up and I still don't know to this day what to do. I just know that I love Chelsie, I love you, and now I want to tell you the rest of what you don't know about me. I still fear how it will end, but I don't know any other way because after the other night, you would constantly wonder why I reacted the way I did without sweeping all of that under the rug. She couldn't stop shaking and crying while she was talking. I had completely gone blank on all I had been digging up about Kira. I was lost on words to say as she was sitting there balling and babbling on.

"You love Chelsie, your niece? Of course you love her, what does she have to do with this?"

Kira wiped her eyes and stared off into the corner of the room for a moment. She took a deep breath and said, "Chelsie is not my niece, she is my daughter."

Then it all had come back to me. I had been so back and forth with stories, I had forgotten this one. "Your daughter," I responded calmly and as though I had no clue.

"She doesn't know it, but yes, she is my daughter, Kyle. She is my daughter and you are the only one that knows it besides my parents. I was so young and stupid, Kyle. I didn't know how to handle the situation back then. I was so young! I had gotten involved with a teacher and coach at the high school I was attending back home before we moved here. I can't honestly tell you how things started but he and I became intimate. I had become so clouded with the idea of thinking that I could be in love with this older man and that he could be in love with me. No one knew, not even my best of friends. He started to give me rides home from school. We started taking pit stops before going home. My parents were so busy with the family business and their social status in the community that they never knew my schedule. Heck, they never really came to any of my games or anything. They never even wondered how I got home from practice. Anyway, our pit stops became long talks, and our long talks started getting intimate. We started spending so much secret time together. I thought he really liked me. Things were fine between us until I had gotten pregnant. I kept it a secret as long as I could before I knew that I would eventually start showing. I confronted him first in hoping that he loved me and that we could run away together. Foolish, I know but it beat telling my parents about the whole situation. I loved my parents and I truly did not want to disappoint my mother or my father. He responded totally different than how I played it out in my mind. He cried about his life and career. He then went on to tell me that he had a fiancé. I began to get so sick and depressed that I didn't show up to school for a week. That is when I had to tell my parents about what was going on. My father was so furious. All he could tell me was my life was ruined and the family reputation was destroyed. He insisted on me having an abortion, but my mother wouldn't have it. My mother couldn't bear the thought, nor wanted me to live with the pain of what it could be like growing up knowing that I killed my child. I remember the call I had gotten from my best friend who was also my teammate. She said Coach Townsend had resigned, quit his job, packed up, and left town with his fiancé overnight. He was gone within the blink of an eye and that was the last I had heard from him. The whole town considered him such a great coach and couldn't figure out why he would give up such a great career and team. No one knew why he resigned and left so suddenly. Only I knew the truth. Coach Edward Townsend, I thought he loved me, but I was just caught up in having someone listen to me. I thought he was truly there for me. I haven't gotten close to anyone since then until now. My parents withdrew me from school and my mother home schooled me until we moved because I had started showing. I never got the opportunity to say goodbye to my friends at school or anything. Like Coach Townsend, we were gone overnight. Once I had Chelsie, my father and mother convinced me to finish school at a private school upstate. I joined the softball team there and later received a scholarship to play at a small college not too far from where I was attending private school. I watched Chelsie grow from afar. My father did his best to make sure I was in her life as little as possible. Since I was sent away, I had been determined to get my life situated, and come back for Chelsie. So I continued to play sports to keep my scholarship, finish school, earn my degree, and come back for Chelsie. As Chelsie grew older, my father fed her that shipwreck story to keep all the confusion down for anyone else who would ask or wonder. I want to tell her but my father insists that is best she doesn't know. He says it will ruin her and make things worse. My parents have custodial rights to Chelsie and I have little money to win her back legally in court. Kyle, I can't play the aunt anymore. That is my daughter and I want her to know that her mother exists and still loves her. I want her to know the truth, but I don't want her to hate me for living this lie. I didn't tell you sooner because I didn't want you to think bad of me and leave me once I had developed these feelings for you. The only time I tried to tell you was that day I met your mother. All the things I said as we walked around the nursing home was me on the inside trying to confess or somehow get you to see the other side of such a story. Once I had known you had been through similar, I felt that there was no way that you would understand what had happened in my past. I still don't know how you will respond but I have been alone all my life and I am prepared to go back to that if you choose to have nothing to do with me anymore. My feelings for you are real. I knew that a story like this would drive you away. Somehow I figured I could fix everything on my own and you would never know. That was just something I had dreamed up in my head. I thought somehow we could be this fairytale family. The hardest reality of it is that I would eventually have to tell you that Chelsie was my daughter. That was the reality of the story that could not be avoided. I kept telling myself that I would wait for the right time to tell you, but the truth is that there is no right time. You just kept on talking about family and future. The more you talked about it the more scared and frustrated I had become. Once it had gotten to the point to where it was time to tell someone about it, I ran from you. I ran from you in fear that you would reject me and that I would be alone again like I have been for so many years. I truly don't want to go back to being alone or fighting for Chelsie alone, but if that is what I'm forced to live with, I will suffer the consequences. I just don't want things to end with us on a bad note and you being left in the dark."

This was the first time I noticed Kira looking me in eyes after telling me the story. Something inside me felt some of the weight had been lifted off her shoulders and that she was no longer hiding anything. I had suspected things weren't right while I was investigating her story. I had also made my mind up that I would be there for her once it unfolded and I will stand on that decision. I just truly don't have the right words to say or any idea on how to fix the issue. I was so determined to get the truth out of her and get things in the open. Now that things are out in the open between us, I felt bad for forcing the issue. I thought I would feel better about the truth coming out, but a part of me feels like a total jerk for pushing her to this point. All I know right now is that I truly care for Kira, and I am going to try and do my best to help her get Chelsie back.

"Oh my goodness, that is a lot to bear for one person. I don't have any good advice to give you right now or know what to do, but I will not leave you alone. I promise that much," I told her as I pulled her into my arms.

"And that is enough for me, Kyle. I didn't want you to go anywhere," she responded as she squeezed a little harder.

She started to calm down and relax after it was all said and done. She went upstairs and got cleaned up. We sat up and had a glass of wine for a little while and headed to bed. It was good to have my Kira back. I had truly missed her while she was gone. I was so worried things were over between us.

Chapter Nine

As I was on my way to work the next morning, I reflected back on everything that had went on last night. My heart was hurting for Kira and all that she had been through up until this point. I could tell that she had felt better after telling me everything by the way she laid in my arms last night before we fell asleep. I meant what I had said about not leaving her. Mother and Mr. Robinson were right. Just because she had a horrible past did not change who I had met and had been dating up until now. The fact that she was afraid to tell me doesn't mean that she is a horrible person or some liar. For the first time, I had placed myself in her shoes. I would be terrified to tell anyone. I would be terrified to try and fix things with my family. More so, I would be terrified in trying to uncover the truth and present it to Chelsie. That was going to be the toughest task she would face, trying to present the truth to Chelsie.

Chelsie had lived most of her life thinking she had no mother and father. Once she hears the truth, she is going to feel that everyone has been lying to her. I imagine that all of this will be hard to process for a teenager. I know at my age now; that if my mother would try to come forth with the truth, it would be hard for me to process as an adult. I don't know if there is any real explanation to explain away the truth and why people did what they did leading up to this point in life. At this point, I was just glad that the truth was out and we could move on to the next phase in our relationship. My first idea was that I needed to talk to my mother and perhaps Mr. Robinson. Those two were great at giving good advice and direction. One thing was for certain, and that is that Kira was going to need all the help she could get in trying smooth things over with her family and Chelsie.

Once I arrived at the nursing home, I went straight to the desk and retrieved my paperwork from Mrs. Sharon as usual. She wasn't there waiting for me this morning, but she did leave my folder in her tray on the desk. It had a posted note with my name written on it. I didn't think much of her not being there. I'm sure everything was all right. I had an attitude of determination today. I was on a mission to get the ball rolling in helping Kira get things straightened out. Plus, I hadn't forgotten about Mr. Robinson and the Jo Anna Kilo mystery also. A part of me couldn't help but to want some clarity on this issue. My gut wants all things to just make sense out of this whole ordeal. I still had planned on getting in touch with Coach Stally in the near future.

Before I went to visit my mother, I stopped by Mr. Robinson's office to check on him. I wanted to know if everything was okay after our trip and conversation. I know it wasn't easy, having to talk about his past issue in losing Ms. Kilo. Once I arrived at his office, the door was shut. I knocked but no one answered and the door was locked. I assume he must have been here in the facility somewhere taking care of an issue of some sort. I proceeded on down to visit my mother for the day. Plus, we had a lot of things to discuss today.

"Knock, knock, anybody home?" I was so excited to see my mother today.

"Here I am, sweetie. Give me a couple of minutes, I am putting the finishing touches on my hair, and I will be right out." I could hear her voice coming from her bedroom. I looked down at my watch because I had found it strange that she was up, getting ready later than usual. Once I looked down at the time, I noticed I was a bit earlier than usual and she wasn't late at all. "To what do I owe this early visit this morning? Is everything all right, dear?"

"Kira finally came back mother. She had finally told me the truth about everything we had been talking about. The girl Chelsie is her daughter. She had gotten involved in an intimate relationship with her high school softball coach when she was a teenager. To make a long story short, she had gotten pregnant and the coach skipped town with his fiancé. Once she had notified her parents, her father became angry, moved the family out of town, and shipped Kira off to private school. The whole story she had given me about Chelsie being her niece is the story that her father had come up with and made her tell Chelsie up until now. Kira is moving back into town to try and get Chelsie back, hoping to fix things."

"My lord Kyle, that's an awful thing that has happened. That's not going to be no easy task for her to accomplish. How are her parents taking all of this?" Mother replied as she reared back in her chair with her hand on her chest.

"I don't think that her father is receiving the news too well. He told Kira that doing such would only make a mess of things and damage Chelsie emotionally. Her mother really doesn't go against her father at all. So the issue is mainly Kira having to deal with her father about telling Chelsie the truth. I was hoping to talk to you and maybe Mr. Robinson on how I may be able to help her."

"So I assume your feelings have changed and you have decided to help Kira? I am glad that you have finally decided to see things in a different light Kyle. Just because people have made some poor choices that may have been influenced by some bad circumstances doesn't make them bad people. Life just has its way of throwing us curve balls and detours. Sometimes we hit homeruns and sometimes we strike out. That was the advice your father used to give people all of the time. He loved using that baseball analogy. The reason he loved it so much is because he would always say that if we happened to strike out numerous times, there would always be another chance at bat again. I learned a lot from Kenneth. He had such an amazing heart, full of grace, and love for people."

Mother smiled as she spoke of Dad. I guess this whole story made her remember some of the words and influence he had on her. "Kyle, the best thing that you can do for Kira is to be there to support her in such a difficult time. This is an issue that she will have to fix with her parents. She can't go at it alone for sure. I am sure the whole thing seems overwhelming to her. I can only imagine what she is up against. I've heard that Mr. Alexander can be a little strange. Kyle, don't try to get too involved to where you may cause an issue with her father and you. This may be the woman you want to marry one day and you don't want to have some bad blood starting out with you and your possible future in-laws. Be there for support, encouragement, and some sort of a resource. That poor girl is going to need a lot of help. I just hope she can solve this thing without having to take any legal matters against her parents. You also let her know that I am here if she needs to stop by at times to vent or get things off her chest. I sure hope things work out as well for Chelsie. I'm sure she would be excited to know that her real mother lives and has always been there for her the whole time. Hopefully she can see pass what happened in the past that caused her mother to be named as her aunt. Every child needs their biological mother and father if they are available or living."

Mother had some great advice. She was certainly right about me not getting too involved in personal affairs between her and her father. I would hate to start out on the wrong foot with any of her family members. Mother's advice also had led me to put myself in Chelsie's shoes. What if my father had come knocking on the door one day telling me that he wasn't my uncle, friend of the family, or co-worker? How would I respond? Would I be relived knowing that my real father lived and was trying to be there for the whole time? I kind of understand the question Kira had asked me in the past. Would it change how I felt? Would I be more forgiving? Mother made good sense today on how influences can lead us to make good and bad choices. Who we are today shouldn't define the poor choices we have made, especially, if we are trying to live better lives. Not only did this talk help me with Kira, but it helped me with my life situation as well. It would take some time, but I think I could be forgiving. I hadn't gotten my hopes up that my father would one day show up on my doorstep begging for forgiveness, but I didn't cause me to look at things from a different perspective. My mother and father abandoned me and that is it. Neither of those two ever came close to even search for me. I bet they are off living their life somewhere with no children. Surely they have learned from their first mistake.

"Thank you so much for the wonderful advice, Mother. I knew I could count on you to give me the much needed direction on how to help Kira in her situation. You and Dad have helped so many people in the past. I hope one day that I could only live up to being a great person like you and my father were."

"Kyle, you are more like your father than you know. I see him in you every time we talk and interact. You have a great heart like your father. You have already grown to be a wonderful man like him as well." My mother hugged me and kissed me on the cheek before I had left to make my way back to my office.

On my way to my office, I stopped back by Mr. Robinson's office. The door was open this time as I entered his office. "Hey, sir, what do you have going on there?" I had come into Mr. Robinson going through what looked like an old photo album of pictures and newspaper clippings. He immediately closed it and placed it back in his desk. Strange how he responded after he had seen my eyes acknowledge the photo album.

"Nothing, son, just going through some old college photos in this old album that Mrs. McCormic had put together for me while I was back in college. I thought about it after our trip this weekend."

"Oh, that's nice. I've got a little time to spare before I get back to my work; let's take a look at it together? What do you say sir?" I really didn't have any time on my hands. I just wanted to get another reaction out of him to make sure I wasn't overthinking how strange he was acting over this photo album.

"Maybe some other time son. I was actually on my way out the door before I had gotten side tracked looking at that old album. I was on my way out for lunch. Would you like to come, my treat?" Mr. Robinson sure acted strange about me wanting to see that album. He was quick to put it away. He even sprang to his feet and proceeded to politely escort me out of his office, locking the door behind us. I knew something was off about this whole situation. I didn't recall ever seeing that album out of all the years he and I had spent together. Mr. Robinson was surely hiding something. I wonder if that album is full of Jo Anna Kilo photographs. I wonder if it's photographs of their relationship during his stay at college. I wonder did mother ever meet Jo Anna Kilo. Two things I must find out for certain—that is, what is in that photo album and what happened to Jo Anna Kilo.

The first order of business was to get in touch with Kira and talk more about how she planned on getting Chelsie back. Things had gotten so strange in an instance that I had actually forgotten that I had stopped by his office to talk to him about what Kira and I had talked about the other night. I immediately forgot by being caught off guard at the sight of him and this photo album. Once again, I couldn't forget how awfully strange he responded to me making notice of that album.

After I finished my days work, I headed home to relax and gather my thoughts. I figured I would call Kira over for dinner or a few drinks. She said that it would be a couple of hours before she could stop by. She was concerned if her coming by so late would be an issue. I didn't want much but a nice conversation over some dinner and a few glasses of wine. So I told her that later would be fine. Plus, it would give me some time to unwind, relax, and process all that had went on today.

Once I had gotten myself cleaned up and the house straightened up to have company; I went into the study to look up the number of the college that Mr. Robinson had attended. My intentions were to contact Coach Stally and do some digging on this Jo Anna Kilo case. I had to get some clarity on the history between Miss. Kilo and Mr. Robinson. I had found the number on the internet. I called the college but Coach Stally wasn't available. I had gotten as far as the athletic department. I left my number and email with some lady that had answered the phone. She said that she would see to it that Mr. Stallons would get my information and message. While I was waiting on Kira to arrive, I had searched the college records for Jo Anna Kilo. Records had shown that she had played basketball in Brazil for eight years, then Italy for another seven. After her fifteen-year career ended, there were no other records indicating where her possible whereabouts would be. I sure hope Coach Stally doesn't get too alarmed by my message and decide to ignore me or blow me off. I sure hope he doesn't contact Mr. Robinson. I don't want Mr. Robinson alarmed about me trying to dig up the past. Which sort of made me think; maybe I should leave the past in the past and not dig any further? Either way, Coach Stally was going to get my message one way or another. What happens next: rest upon whether he decides to contact me or not to talk about the issue?

I could finally see the head lights of Kira's car shining through the study window. I rose out of my chair to go let her in the front door. When I opened the door, she was coming up the step with two large brown paper sacks. "Hey, sweetie, I hope you haven't started dinner yet. I figured I would grab some Chinese takeout with it being so late and all. I wouldn't want to spend what little time we had together tonight cooking and working around the kitchen. I wasn't too sure on what you actually liked, so I got a little bit of a variety for you to pick and choose from. Hopefully, I did pick out something in here that you would like. I wanted to surprise you at the least." I grabbed one of the bags from her arms at the door and we proceeded to make our way in the kitchen. I thought to myself that she couldn't really go wrong with Chinese on the go. I loved takeout. There wasn't really too much that I didn't eat as far as takeout was concerned.

"All of it smells good that's for sure. You just pick out what you want to eat and I will work from there dear." She sure did pick up a little bit of everything. She had my house smelling like a buffet.

"How was your day today at work, Kyle? Did you get to see your mother? I really enjoy her company and conversation. She is truly a remarkable woman." I didn't even have to ask if Kira had a good day. She was in good spirits as we prepared to dig in and eat. She had this glow of happiness about her tonight. I hadn't seen this much glow since our first night that we met.

"Yes, I saw my mother today. She and I had a nice little conversation between mother and son. She is truly something special. I don't know where I would be without her love. I am thankful that God has placed her in my life. She is a great mother and friend. I know we all have to pass on to the next life one day, but I hope that day is far off in the future. I love that woman with all of my heart." I couldn't imagine what life would be like without mother. I couldn't imagine my day to day at work, not being able to visit her like I always do. I couldn't fathom what life would be like with her smile and personality in my everyday life. "How did things go today with you and your mother?"

"She and I had a heart to heart as well. We went browsing for some house hold knick-knacks that she had in mind for decorating her kitchen. I swear that woman decorates that kitchen every year. Then we went out to eat. I had taken her to Alice's Café. I had requested the both that you and I had sat in the first night we met. We ate and sat there for hours drinking coffee and talking about future plans of me living her in town. I did tell her that I had met a very nice man, and that we had been dating for some time now. I told her how we met and how you had brought me to the same spot we were dining in. I told her about the wedding and how nice your family was. She said she had heard of the McComic family. She mainly talked about your Uncle Kevin and your cousin Marcus. She talked about the construction business and how popular Marcus was in football. She didn't say too much about knowing your mother and father. She said all she knew was from the reputation your family had in town. She said that she had never met any of them face-to-face. We were going on and on about you like two little high school girls. She seemed very happy for me." As Kira was talking, you could see the excitement in her eyes and hear it in her voice. I was glad that she and her mother had a great day and were able to talk about some personal things going on in Kira's life. I didn't want to ask if she had told her mother that her new man was black, but I couldn't help myself.

"Did you tell your mother that not only was I handsome, but that I was black also? That generally scares most Caucasian parents," I said it with sarcasm in my voice hoping to lighten the subject and to keep the laughter flowing.

Kira immediately spit out some of her drink as she burst into laughter. "Actually I did, Kyle. I did tell her that you were a very attractive black man. I told her that you were the first black man that I had ever dated. You are actually the first black man that has ever approached me. I thought that she may be alarmed by it as well before I decided to let her know, but the conversation kept flowing. She was doing her best to get me to describe you. She even went on to ask me were you handsome like some of the Hollywood black actors she and I have seen on TV. The whole conversation about you was mind blowing as I listened to her go on and on pressing me to tell her more about you and me." I could tell Kira was excited how her mother received her dating a black man. I could tell she felt some sort of relief in being able to talk to her mother.

"How does your mother feel about you moving back in town and spending more time with Chelsie?" I knew this was going to be no easy take, and I am sure Kira was aware that it wasn't going to be easy neither. I just wanted to be aware of what she was up against and where I should try to focus on helping her the most.

"Mother is excited about me moving back to town. We do talk about telling Chelsie the truth. My father is the one that needs convincing. Mother doesn't want to disrupt any peace between her and my father, but she definitely agrees with me about telling Chelsie the truth. It's not going to be easy trying to convince my father on telling Chelsie the truth, but it will take everyone's support in getting everything out in the open for things to go smoothly. She believes that it will be hard for Chelsie to understand why everyone kept things a secret at first; and I agree with her on that subject. I think we all should have told the truth in the beginning, but my father is the one that created the lie. He doesn't want to lose Chelsie's trust in him. I just don't agree with it being at the expense of her never knowing who her real mother is. He should have never told this lie in the first place. Sometimes I just feel like giving up Kyle and living with things the way they are, but I want my daughter to know that I am her mother and that I love her more than the world itself. I just put the family and her in a bad situation and I am sorry for that. This whole mess is all, my fault." Kira's eyes started to form tears as she was venting about telling the Chelsie the truth and having to face her dad. She wiped her eyes, walked over to the island, poured herself a drink, and returned to her seat at the dining room table. I got and moved my chair closer to her and placed my hand on top of hers.

"I know it's not going to be easy, honey. I'm sure that things will work out. You just can't give up now. I think it is a wonderful thing you are doing in pursuing this relationship with your daughter. We've just got a mountain in our way that we need to climb. No, it's not going to be easy but you don't have to go at it alone. I am here with you and I will do my best to endure with you all the way."

Kira leaned over and placed her head on my shoulder after I finished talking.

"Thank you, Kyle. I just can't wait to get through with all of this so everyone can move on with life. I'm just ready to get started with the next chapter in my own life. The page won't turn until Chelsie knows that I am her mother and hopefully we can continue to grow closer." Kira was sad, but she seemed at ease knowing that she had my support and a little of her mother's support in the matter. She was right, though; her father was going to be no easy task. I was glad I could help. I didn't tell her that she had mother's support too because I didn't know how comfortable she would feel about me telling mother the whole story. I wonder how her father is going to take me being black as well. Kira and I finished eating, cleaned up the kitchen, and watched a little bit of television in the living room before she went home.

CHAPTER TEN

I had gotten up a little early the next day. I had to run by the drugstore to pick up mother's medicine before I headed into work. "Good morning, Mrs. Thomas, how are you doing this morning?" Mr. and Mrs. Thomas were both pharmacists that ran the town's local drugstore. It was the only one in town. Everyone in the town got all of their medicine from the "Thomas Family Pharmacy."

"I'm doing all right, Mr. McCormic. I assume you are here for your mother's prescription? I called you yesterday and left a message. I knew you would be in today to get your mother's medicine, but it will be in tomorrow morning. I'm terribly sorry, but we don't have the prescription filled today." Mrs. Thomas kept apologizing repeatedly, but it was truly no big deal. Mother had enough left to keep her into next week. We just generally picked up the medicine early so she would have it on hand as soon as she ran out.

"No worries, Mrs. Thomas, I will just stop by tomorrow morning on my way to work. She has plenty to keep her into next week. Don't stress yourself over it, please?"

"I will try not to, Mr. McCormic. Your mother has been so good to the community and our local business, I kind of feel as it being a disservice to her. Did she ever tell you that your father and your uncle built this drugstore for me and my husband after we had graduated college? The banks would not approve us for any business loans after we had accumulated so much college debt. Mr. Thomas and I had a passionate desire to open a drugstore in this community, but we couldn't get the funds together. We had saved up a little bit of money, but certainly not enough to get a business started. Mr.

Thomas and I started working for the old town's drugstore before this one. The owner of the previous drugstore had gotten older and was ready to retire after his wife had passed. He was going to sell his drugstore, retire, and do some traveling before he found somewhere to settle down. What little money Cliff and I had saved up surely wasn't enough for any retirement. The man that bought the drugstore decided to open up a local hardware store. Cliff and I had surely not attended college to work in some local hardware, so our only option was to move until I had met your mother one day in the store before it closed. She was concerned with what Cliff and I would do once the store closed and the hardware store had opened. I explained our situation, and all that we had planned to her that day. I had no idea that she would be such a blessing from God that day. The following week, your father contacted the store looking for me and my husband. We had met your father and your uncle for lunch that day, and they both presented us with a business plan. They said that they would take care of everything; all we had to do was give them the little money we had saved up as a down payment and pay them back as much as we could as time passed and business progressed. Your mother and your father helped us with a business plan also. It didn't take long for this drugstore to flourish in this town. The people were so nice and helpful with the support of the McCormic family. Cliff and I have been able to pay off all our college debt and raise a beautiful family. Every year, Cliff and I deposit a little money into an account of Brenda's to show our gratitude and appreciation. God has truly used the McCormic family to bless so many people in this town. Once again, I am sorry that we didn't have her prescription filled. We will certainly have it in tomorrow. Let your mother know that I said hello and not a day goes by that we don't think about what Kenneth and Brenda did for the Thomas family."

"I certainly will let Mother know, Mrs. Thomas. Once again, don't stress too hard over the delay. I will see you in the morning." Mrs. Thomas gave me a hug and kiss on the cheek as she escorted me out of the front entrance of the pharmacy. As I drove to work, I continued to think about the story that Mrs. Thomas had told me. I wasn't surprised that my family built the drugstore. I was blessed by the story that Mrs. Thomas had told me about how my parents had helped them get the business started. That story made me even more proud of my mother and father. I couldn't wait to get to work and talk to mother about the story I've heard this morning.

Once I had gotten work, there wasn't any paperwork waiting for me at the front desk. I thought Mrs. Sharon was slacking on her work today, but she informed me that there wasn't anything to hand out for me today. I reckon I could take the day off, but I just had to see mother in my free time before I left for the day.

"Knock, knock, pretty lady." Mother came out of her room to greet me as I entered her quarters. She looked beautiful as always. I grabbed her, gave her a big hug, and kissed her on the cheek. I looked her in her eyes and told her how proud I was of her.

"Well, you sure know how to start an old woman's morning off. What has gotten into you this morning?" Mother reared back and laughed at how she was greeted. We then proceeded to the kitchen as she started fixing breakfast.

"They didn't have your prescription filled this morning at the drugstore. I had an interesting conversation with Mrs. Thomas this morning. She told me how you and dad helped her get the drugstore started. Dad told me they built it, but never told me the story in behind it."

"Your father and I never believed it was right to tell everything we've done for people. We never wanted to seem like we were bragging or boasting about helping others. We done quite a few acts of kindness here and there for others, but we always kept it to ourselves. Keeping score never was our thing. You have some people out there that have done things for others or do things for others, and just brag or boast about it every chance they get. I don't know why people have to make sure they remind others of what they have done or notify people around them of what they are doing. Blessing others was always between us and God. Well, the people we blessed also, but we never broadcasted anything in the community. That's one of the main reasons I fell in love with Kenneth. He believed he could use that construction business to build a better world around him. He and Kevin believed in blessing others with what God had blessed them with. When God speaks of overflow in our lives; he doesn't mean for it to be wasted and spilled out to be misused. He wants us to bless others. Your father believed in not wasting one drop of his overflow from God. That man's faith in God was truly extraordinary. He taught me a lot. I wasn't all that much of a believer when I met your father. I attended church enough to keep the members off my back when I didn't show up. I knew about God, but I didn't know God like your father did when we met. Your father introduced me to God. Observing your father and his relationship with God took my faith to another level. I knew this was a phenomenal man, and if I was going to keep him, I had better get onboard with Jesus." Mother laughed as she said that. "Your father taught me about the things of God. His father was a minister. Although the children didn't follow in their father's footsteps, the apples didn't fall too far from the tree. Your father and uncle taught me that people were the bricks that built this community. One person at a time was one brick at a time and it worked."

Mother was right about Dad. I remember how he would tell me about God. Those stories he told me when I was younger stuck with me through college on up until now. My friends and I all attended the same church. I don't remember papaw. Dad said he had passed away when I was four years old. We still attended the same church under the new pastor. Most of the town attended that church. Dad told me that his father built that church. He and Uncle Kevin later rebuilt that church not too long after their father passed away.

"Kira and I had dinner last night. We talked about Chelsie and her mother. Kira did tell her mother about me and that I was black." I changed the subject, but this was what I had intended on sharing with mother before my episode at the drugstore this morning.

"Well, that was a surprise. I didn't expect to go from one extreme to another. How did that go?" I could tell how shocked mother was at change in subject. Also, the look of concern about me being black was written all over her face.

"She said her mother is onboard with her telling Chelsie the truth. Her father is the one that will need convincing that it is the right thing to do. Surprisingly her mother is thrilled at the thought of me being black. She said her mother never showed any concern for Kira being white and me being black. I myself was relieved to hear that one. You could tell mother still had some concern about it.

"I'm glad that things are going smooth so far. Mothers generally don't have the issue of interracial relationships, it's mainly the fathers. I hope Mr. Alexander doesn't overstep his boundaries with my son. Kyle, you be careful with him. I don't know him personally, but he still hasn't come into the picture yet and I am not too sure about him from all that I have heard. I haven't heard of him being racist or anything, but this is his daughter. Not everyone sees things the same as other people do." Mother was right. I didn't feel like everything was totally in the clear with the Alexanders on this interracial relationship with Kira. I would feel comfortable if Mr. Alexander wasn't okay with it. Something on the inside tells me he won't be and may try to make things difficult. Other than that issue, I planned on moving forward on helping Kira get her daughter back.

Mother finished cooking. She and I decided to change the subject to something more comfortable to talk about as we finished eating breakfast. I helped her clean up the kitchen and then headed home. I stopped by the grocery store on the way home. The kitchen stock was running a little low and needed replenishing. After I had gotten all the groceries in, I called up the crew to see if they wanted to meet at the Hole in the Wall later. Everybody decided to meet up later this evening. I even invited Kira. She said that she would drive to my house so she and I could ride together in the same vehicle. I told her not to dress up because we were all headed out to the Hole in the Wall for wings, pizza, and sports. Football ball was ending with a few games left and basketball was beginning. I was lucky that Kira loved sports. It was nice that I could finally have someone that I could take around the guys and she actually fit in.

Kira had showed up a little early. She said that she wanted to pick out one of my hooded sweatshirts to wear to the restaurant tonight. She picked out one of my Highland Vikings hooded sweatshirts to wear. It looked fairly large on her, but she did look cute in it. Things had really progressed between us. The ride over was even different. Kira had taken my hand and placed it on her thigh the whole trip over. The radio station seemed to be playing all of our favorite old school jams that she and I claimed to have listened to back when we were in school. She looked so cute singing along with the songs as they came on across the radio. I even joined in on a few that I called myself knowing the words to as well. Once we arrived, I didn't take long for us to get seated. Kira and Jacs sat closer toward the end of the table down from me and the fellas. The two were having their own conversation while the guys were laughing and joking throughout the night. It seemed like everyone could use a night out and let loose. We all ended up staying long enough to close the place down.

Kira and I had finally made it back to my place. It was awfully late, so I offered Kira to crash at my place until I had to leave for work in the morning. "I had such a great night tonight that I honestly do not want it to end. Why don't you just crash here tonight since it so late? That way you don't have to drive home and lose any rest you could be getting." That was a clever way of me asking her to spend the night.

"I don't see any harm in Kira staying the night. You just make sure you behave yourself Mr. McCormic," Kira replied with sarcasm as she got out of the car and made her way toward the front door. She went up stars and found an old T-shirt and some athletic shorts of mine to wear to bed. Before we knew it, we were in the bed, and off to sleep before either of us could get another word in.

CHAPTER ELEVEN

The next morning, I was awakened an hour earlier than my alarm by my phone. I had received an email. The email was from Coach Stally. He had said that he had gotten my message from the woman who had answered the phone that day. He told me that he would be available to meet me and John halfway for lunch in a couple of days if that was something we would like to do. I replied telling him that we would be glad to meet him halfway for lunch. He gave me the name of the restaurant to meet him at in his reply to my email. Little did he know was that I would be the only one showing up for lunch. I sent him a message asking did he want to meet up for lunch sometime and play catch up. I knew he would never go for me asking him to meet up and answer some questions about the history between Mr. Robinson and Jo Anna Kilo. Plus I don't want Mr. Robinson to know about me snooping around in his business. I didn't feel comfortable doing so, but I couldn't help wanting to know the whole story.

After I finished emailing Coach Stally, I got up, fixed Kira and myself some breakfast, got a shower, and got dressed for work. She hadn't gotten up yet, so I left her a note by her plate on the table. I figured it couldn't hurt anything for her to sleep in a little longer. Surely she wasn't going to bother or steal anything from the house. I poured myself a cup of coffee before I got ready to leave, grabbed my coat, and hurried out the door.

I hadn't forgotten that I needed to stop by the drugstore to pick up mother's medicine. Mrs. Thomas said that it should be in this morning, hopefully she was right. "Good morning, Mrs. Thomas, did my mother's medicine arrive this morning?"

"It sure did, Mr. McCormic. I have Mrs. Brenda's prescription filled and ready for you. Just give me a second and I will be right back." Mrs. Thomas walked to the back to retrieve mother's prescription. I browsed around while I waited, but Mrs. Thomas didn't take too long. "Here you go, Kyle, sorry for the inconvenience." Mrs. Thomas handed me the medicine over the counted with her usual warm bright smile.

As I walked out of the pharmacy, I heard the voice of an unfamiliar man following me out the door. "McCormic, Kyle McCormic I suppose is your name?" I turned to address the stranger as I did not recognize his face. He was an older Caucasian male, white hair, clean-shaved, and an inch or two taller than I was.

"Yes, sir, I am Kyle McCormic. And you are?" I extended my hand as I addressed him. He looked down and did not extend his in return. An uncomfortable feeling came over me as I couldn't place the face but assumed I was standing in the presence of...

"Alexander, Mason Alexander, I'm Kira's father." The pit grew in my stomach as my mind became bombarded with thoughts of caution, intimidation, and a bit of anger. I thought to myself by the way he didn't accept my gesture that this wasn't going to go well. As I looked back into his eyes, I thought about how his own daughter was afraid to approach him over the issue of getting her daughter back. I could understand why she was so afraid in the first few seconds of standing in his presence. "My wife was telling me about this Kyle McCormic that my daughter had been dating. I didn't suspect that I would be meeting you so soon. It seems as though she has taken quite some liking to a man of your statue."

I guess that was his way of nicely referring to the color of my skin. He looked me up and down and took another small step forward. I didn't retreat or step back. I couldn't understand yet believe his whole demeanor toward me during the time he was talking. "I'm sure she has told you that she is moving back to town. I'm sure you two have plans on continuing to pursue this relationship further. I even bet she told you about her daughter, hasn't she? How do you think Chelsie would respond to the news of Kira being her actual mother, but portraying the role of an aunt for fifteen years? Then to receive more tragic news on how she was brought into this world, abandoned by a father who didn't even want her to be born? Now to be introduced to her real mother's new shell of a man? You think that would go over well?"

I couldn't deny giving some sort of thought to what he was saying. I surely didn't want to cause any trouble for Kira and Chelsie. I didn't want to start out with Kira's father on the wrong foot neither, but he wasn't making things easy on me by his introduction at this moment. Soon the intimidation had left me. I became offended by his somewhat subliminal prejudice approach. I was ready to take him by the throat and drive him through the moniker on the plate glass window of the pharmacy. My chest filled itself with hot air. My fists clinched themselves tightly in my coat pockets. I couldn't remember the last time I was approached in a way that made me want to stomp stupid the man standing in front of me. Rage filled my thoughts as he continued to politely insult me in his own ignorant way. I began to stare back deeper into his eyes letting him know that I wasn't afraid. Without saying a word, I'm sure he could now sense the reality of me not being intimidated by his shrewd comments. Although animosity was brewing in my heart, I made no attempt to escalate things any further.

"I understand how you feel, sir. I'm sure things are a little uneasy with the whole idea of Kira wanting to square things away with her daughter after all this time. I promise you that my intentions are good and to have the upmost respect toward you and your daughter. Kira and I have grown extremely close. I care for her deeply. I would never cross any line to bring any trouble to you or your family. I hope that you and Kira can come to an understanding that better benefits everyone involved. Hopefully somewhere deep down inside you can understand things from Kira's position in the matter. I wish you the best sir. I'm sure we will see each other again someday soon, but I must be going now. I don't want to be late for work or delay in getting my mother what I had come here to get for her. Have a good day, sir!" I disengaged with Mr. Alexander and walked passed him to get in my car and head to work. He never replied after I had said what I said. As I drove away, I could see him standing there on the side walk until he was no longer in sight of my mirror.

After I had arrived to work and got my day started; I couldn't help but to sit in my office and think what a jerk he was. Part of me felt good about standing my ground and not causing any hard issue between Mr. Alexander and myself. The pride in me wished I had annihilated that old man right there on that side walk in front of that pharmacy. He didn't even know me. He wasn't even trying to know me. I didn't want to worry mother with what went on this morning, but I knew that I would eventually have to drop off this medicine. It was inevitable that she and I will have a conversation on the matter. I just couldn't hide the look of concern on my face. As I stared at my mother's pill bottle in front of me on my desk; the whole episode kept replaying itself over and over in my head.

"How's it going today, son?" Just like that my thoughts were interrupted by a knock on the open door of my office. It was Mr. Robinson standing there in good spirits and all smiles. Immediately my whole demeanor changed to keep him from suspecting anything was bothering me.

"Today started off pretty good sir. Kira stayed all night again. I woke up this morning, showered, fixed breakfast, and left her sleeping in back at my place. She should be waking up by now to breakfast and a sweet note from yours truly," as I laughed, putting on a quick façade.

"Well, it sure sounds like things are looking up for the two of you." Mr. Robinson entered my office and sat himself at my desk across from me. "Have you found out anymore on her and her niece or daughter?" I kept my composer, but I thought to myself, *How could he be so worried with what she might be hiding with all the secrets he's been keeping here lately?* I thought to myself, *How about you come clean with your story before you worry about someone else's?*

"Yes, sir, it pans out that Chelsie is her daughter. Kira and I had a good heart to heart on the issue a few days ago. She plans on doing all that she can to establish the truth between her and Chelsie. The hardest part is getting all of her family onboard with the idea of coming clean and introducing the young girl to truth and explaining why she was led to believe the story she had been living for so long. Kira is mainly concerned on how her father will respond to the whole idea of clearing the air. I did assure her that I wouldn't interfere with her family issue, but I would be in her corner supporting all the way. I think that gave her some comfort in knowing that the truth didn't run me off or cause me to push her away.

"You're a good man, son. I knew you would eventually see things from a different perspective. You've always had a good heart. I'm not saying that you had to stay regardless, but I'm glad you took the effort and energy to understand what she may be going through. We don't always make the best choices. All of us have some sort of ugly past that has been written. You and I know that we can't undo what has already been done. We can't rewrite the past, but we can write out the future. Lord knows I've got some things in my past I wish I could fix."

Yeah, I wonder what that could be. Would it have anything to do with what went on in college between you and Jo Anna Kilo? Maybe you can start by telling me why you have been acting the way you have been acting. Perhaps start out by showing that photo album you didn't want to see the other day. Those were the thoughts that crossed my mind as I was listening to him make that last statement. This morning's escapade with Mr. Alexander has me in a mood to just unleash on everybody today. "Well son, I'm glad things are getting better for you. I won't hold you up any longer. Just wanted to stop by and see how my favorite guy was doing. I just know that I haven't seen you in a couple of days. Just know that my door is always open."

"I appreciate it, sir. I will stop by soon for a game of chess here in the near future. Maybe you and I can have one of talks like we always do?"

"Sounds great, son, I would love that." I bet you would love just that. I wonder how much you would love to go through that album with me and tell me about your old "college days." Regardless of whether he was going to tell me or not, I was surely going to get to the bottom of his story soon. Then he would have no choice but to tell me the truth once I present it to him. I felt bad, but couldn't help myself. I was itching to know the truth about Jo Anna Kilo.

After I walked Mr. Robinson back to his office, I made my way down to my mother's room to deliver her medicine. She was sitting in her recliner when I entered her quarters. She was going through some old photo albums while she was sitting there. I placed her medicine in one of the kitchen cabinets that she usually kept all of her meds in.

"How's everything going today mother? Is that the project you have been working on here lately?" Hoping she would say yes and let me in on what she had claimed to have been up to all of these years. I was curious to know what this lifelong project was that she had never mentioned anything about. Seemed like so many people around had so many secrets.

"No, dear, I was just sitting here going through some of our old family photos from the holidays and family get gatherings." Mother had left her recliner, came over, and sat next to me on the coach. "Here, let's take a look at them together. I was hoping you would show up on time this morning so that you and I could look as some of these." Mother began to point at certain photos laughing as she slowly turned the pages. It was amazing how mother had put together all of these albums. There were so many memories on every page. I loved the holidays and family gatherings growing up in the McCormic household. There were photos of all of the family plus the town folk also. I noticed how Mr. Robinson never missed a gathering of family holiday. I assume the McCormics were the only family that he truly had after his mother abandoned him and him not having much to do with his father. I remember how I used to get birthday and Christmas gifts from him every year. Every turn of the page warmed my heart as mother and I turned back the hands of time with her wonderful album projects that she had accumulated over the years up until now. I couldn't stop thinking about Mr. Robinson's mysterious album off and on as we looked through all of mother's albums.

"Mother, did Mr. Robinson ever mention a Jo Anna Kilo during his time in college?" There it was. I had to ask if mother had known anything about his relationship with Jo Anna Kilo. She paused for a moment as she looked to be gathering her thoughts or trying to remember if she could recall every knowing anything about Jo Anna Kilo.

"I remember that name. I believe they were close while he attended college. Kenneth and I met her a few times as we would visit from time to time when John would have home games. She was a nice young lady. She was just as passionate about basketball as John was. Kenneth and I had the opportunity to see her play a couple of times when the women's team would play before the men at home games. John would sit in the stands with Kenneth and myself, and watch her play. We didn't hear much more about her after John had come home for good from college. I imagine it was heartbreaking for John when they had split up. She loved basketball more than to settle down and have a relationship with John. John came home a broken man when he left college. He was a little lost without basketball. Basketball was going to be his number one means of income. He had promised Kenneth and me that once he turned pro, we would want for nothing. He was dead set on repaying us for all he claimed we had done for him. We loved John as our own son. We didn't see things like he did. Although we understood how he felt. That's why you see him in most of all the photos. He stayed here all of the time. All his father ever cared about was the money he would bring home. It had gotten so bad for him with his father, that he would just go home to visit for an hour or two to make sure things were at least taken care of for his father. He would drop off what little money he would give him and return home. We were all he had. The town loved to watch him play basketball. He worked for the construction company during the summers in high school. He had truly become a son to the McCormics. He and I used to keep albums like these all the time just like me and you did when you were coming up. Photo albums have always been special to the McCormic family. They are our own story books in weird sort of way.

"Did you get to see all of the albums, mother? Was there any of him in college?" I was really searching to see if she had come across the album he was hiding from me. I wanted to know why it was so important for him to hide that one from me.

"I don't really know if I had seen all of them. John is a grown man. He didn't spend every moment with Kenneth and me. I am sure he has made some of his own from having a life in college dear. Why are you asking me these questions, Kyle?" Mother had finally caught on as she looked me in the eyes. I could no longer hide what I was thinking. Hopefully she wouldn't alarm Mr. Robinson after I tell her what is bothering me.

"The other day, I had stopped by to see Mr. Robinson. He was going through an old photo album in his office. It alarmed him when I showed up by surprise. He immediately put it away so that I could not see it. When I asked him if we could look through it, he changed the subject and blew me off. Mother, he has never acted that way. We have always gone over old newspaper clippings and photos of his time in school. I can't help to continue to wonder why this album in so important to not let me see it. He has been acting strange ever since he and I went to the basketball game at his old college. We had walked the trophy case in the hall outside the gymnasium after the game. That case was full of photos of Mr. Robinson and Jo Anna Kilo. He told me that they were an item back in college, but no more than that. He told me how she chose not to pursue a relationship with him after he could no longer play basketball. I could tell it hurt him to think about it while we were on the topic. He also ran into an old friend that he used to be teammates with in college. They went off to have a private conversation for a while, but Mr. Robinson never told me what they had talked about. Things have been so strange with him since we returned after that night. I just want to help him, that's all."

"I know you do, dear. I know you want to help John. I'm sure he will get around to opening up and telling you everything. You too are very close. I'm sure he will eventually tell you about whatever it is that he is feeling or going through. Just be patient with him. Try to understand what he may be going through like you did with Kira. So whatever it may be, you are willing to be there for him and listen. We all have some things that have happened in our past that we wish we could rewrite. Just make sure you don't forget what wonderful relationship you two had before he decides to tell you whatever it is that may be bothering him." Mother was right once again. Mr. Robinson had never truly hidden anything from me. I'm sure that stroll down memory lane probably was hard for him to travel down. He and I did have a wonderful relationship. Mother's talk kind of made me feel bad about how hard pressed I was on finding out about that album and this whole Jo Anna Kilo story. I've just been so hard pressed trying to fix everything and help everybody that I might have ended up causing a mess between he and me. I am glad that I did open up to mother and talk to her about it first. Lord knows what I would have caused if I had just up and threw the whole story in his face. I'm sure whatever the story may be, he will tell me in his own time.

"You're right, Mother. Maybe I am being too hard on Mr. Robinson. Thank you for the advice. There is one more thing I had stopped by to talk to you about before I got side tracked on Mr. Robinson. I ran into Mr. Alexander this morning at the pharmacy while I was picking up your prescription. Our first meeting wasn't too pleasant. He was a real jerk. Not to mention, I don't think he is too thrilled about his daughter being involved with a black man. The whole time he stood there talking, I wanted to stomp him stupid. I just know he is going to try and make things worse for Kira on the count of me." My heart was hurting at the thought of having to leave Kira alone in order for her to have some peace between her and her father. The thought of that had never crossed my mind until the episode he and I had this morning.

"Wow, he didn't say anything to hurt you, did he? Did he put his hands on you?" Mother has never been the aggressive type or the one to display anger, although I could tell she was deeply concerned. She and dad were not the fighting type. Uncle Kevin was pretty much the one that would jump on somebody if you pushed him far enough.

"No, he didn't say too much or put his hands on me, but I got the message loud and clear."

"Interracial relationships are new to some people, dear. He doesn't know how wonderful of a man you are. I'm not taking up for him or anything because that certainly doesn't give him the right to act the way he acted this morning. Just stick to the plan of working from the outside and helping Kira. Don't forget that your main focus is on helping Kira get her daughter back. I am sure she feels just as deeply for you as you do for her. Just make sure you stay clear of that old man. I would hate to have to have a talk with him over my son." Mother made sense in what she was saying, but Kira and I would eventually have to cross that bridge sooner or later.

"Thanks, Mother, you always have the best advice for every situation." I meant every word I had said. There have been countless times I've talked to her and she has never been wrong in her assessments of every situation. "It's getting late, and I need to get my work finished before I leave for the day. I will see you tomorrow, I love you."

"Patience, dear, your father taught me patience and how to try and see the good in every situation. You take care, I will see you tomorrow, love you more!" I kissed her on the cheek before I left. The talk with mother today had made things a little easier for both issues concerning Kira and Mr. Robinson. I soon returned to my office, finished my work, and headed home for the day.

CHAPTER TWELVE

I noticed Kira's car was still in the driveway when I arrived. I could smell food cooking and hear music playing when I entered the house. Kira was up and at it. I could tell she been doing a little straightening up in the living room. She was bent over, taking bread out of the oven when I entered the kitchen.

"Good afternoon, sweetie. How was your day?" She was obviously in a good mood. She had on some sweat pants and the T-shirt she slept in last night. My guess is that she has been here all day.

"I had a very interesting day today, dear," I replied as I smiled into her eyes as she placed her arms around my neck and greeting me with a kiss. I wonder if I should tell her about my episode with her father this morning. I really didn't want to ruin the moment we were having. It felt good coming home to her and especially seeing her in such a good mood. I didn't want to lose this moment. In my mind it felt like a preview of what life with Kira could be like, plus a Chelsie somewhere in the house. There was plenty of space and land here for more than just me.

"Well, I'm willing to hear all about it later if you are willing to share it over dinner and wine. I hope you like spaghetti. I went rumbling through your cabinets and found all the ingredients. I have been here all day. I woke up late this morning. I got your note and your breakfast. I thought it was very sweet of you. Breakfast taste better when someone you care for prepares it for you. After I had eaten, I had taken a shower then decided that I would just spend the day here. I straightened up a little around the house; then decided I would stick around and get dinner ready for when you arrived. I don't know what has gotten into me today. Everything just felt like I was supposed to be here and I didn't want to leave feeling that way. So I stayed and here we are." I was glad she stayed. Things did feel in place with her being here. Even with everything that has been going on today, I felt worry free for the time being. Kira was someone I could truly see myself spending the rest of my life with.

Once we finished dinner, we cleaned up the kitchen and retired to the living room cuddled on the couch watching whatever we could find on the television. Things had finally started to get quiet, so I decided it was a good enough time to tell her what had happened this morning. "About my day today, I had run into your father this morning at the pharmacy." Kira sprang up from the position she was in laying my stomach.

"What did he say? How did he know it was you? How did it go?" She went from content to worried, in the matter of a second.

"He was a little forward. That is a polite way of saying it. He didn't seem too thrilled about you dating me. I could tell my skin color was bothering him. He mentioned how he wasn't too comfortable with you wanting to tell Chelsie the truth. He said that even if you all agreed to do such a thing that Chelsie would have an even bigger issue with having a black man as a possible stepfather. I could tell that he was doing his best to get his point across without making a scene in front of the drugstore. It made me think a little. I started to feel that maybe your life would be easier without all the issues of interracial dating on top of what you are going through. I thought that, until I talked to my mother about it after I had arrived to work. Mother said that I should continue on with you and focus on helping you get your daughter back. That should be the main focus for now and worry about our pursuit of a deeper relationship after all that is squared away. She said I should remain in your corner for support. I admit that she did make a lot of sense. I just don't want you worried or cause any more stress on you than you already have."

Kira then calmed down and returned to laying her head on my stomach. "I agree with your mother. I like her perspective most of all. I hate that all this has happened. I had no idea he would be so concerned with skin color. I had no idea that he would be so difficult about who I chose to date as long as that person was good to me and treated me nice. I am deeply sorry for what you went through this morning. I didn't know that he would be such a jerk to you. I am grateful that you decided to stick around and remain with me. Kyle, I care about you a lot. I am serious about it when I tell you that this is where I want to be and a serious relationship is something that I want to pursue with you. As for Chelsie, I don't think she will have an issue at all with you and me dating. She and I talk about this boy she has a crush on at school. She hasn't said anything to him, but they do spend a lot of time together at school. He plays on the football and basketball team, and he so happens to be black. My parents just don't know about it yet. So if my father has an issue with interracial relations, I will be the least of his problems. I plan on telling Chelsie here soon about her being my daughter. I plan on telling her with or without my father's permission. She is my daughter and I am her mother and that is just what it is. It is not up to him to determine whether she and I should have a mother-daughter relationship or not. I imagine it must have been difficult to tell me this with all that is going on in both of our lives, but I am glad you did. I'm glad you trusted me with it." Kira had put my mind at ease about the whole ordeal. I was glad I told her. I was surprised at how the talk about her father's behavior this morning turned out. I am just glad that she decided for us to stick together. She was right. Chelsie is her daughter and she has the right to know the truth. It's a huge mountain to climb, but I am sure God will help put things in the order they need to be in. Kira and I didn't say much for the rest of the night. We just laid there and watched television until it was time to go to bed. I could tell that she was still a little worried, but I kept comforting her with hugs and reassuring her that everything will work out for the good of everyone involved.

When I woke up the next morning, Kira had already been gone. Breakfast and a note, was left on the table as usual. I ate, showered, and headed out the door for work. I wasn't going to spend too much time at work today. I had plans to meet Coach Stally half way for lunch. He was still under the impression that he was meeting Mr. Robinson and me for lunch. I sure hope all of this doesn't blow up in my face and cause any division between Mr. Robinson and me. I would hate for us not to be as close because I went behind his back on something like this. I thought to myself that it might be better to cancel the lunch with Coach Stally and take another approach at cracking the case. Part of me felt like it was too late to turn back now on the lunch with Coach Stally. If anything, I won't say nothing about it and just have lunch with the man.

Today turned out to be a perfect day to sneak away unsuspected. Mr. Robinson had decided to take Mother out for lunch and a little shopping. He said it had been a while since he had treated her to a nice day out. Every so often he would take Mother out for the day. He would treat her to dinner or lunch, stroll through the park, take her for a drive, and even to the mall for a little shopping. He had been doing this ever since he had gotten his job and rental properties started. He said he will never forget what they had done for him and that it was part of his own way of showing his gratitude for all they had done. He used to take mother and father both up until dad passed away. He still continued to do so long after dad passed. Mother loved the treatment as well. She said that John had made a promise to dad before he died that he would treat her to the things that she enjoyed. She said it was part of dad still taking care of her in his own way after he was gone.

While they were away, I snuck on down the high way to meet Coach Stally for lunch. I figured I would get there a little early so he wouldn't see me getting out of the car without Mr. Robinson. I had the waiter seat me closer toward the back of the restaurant so he couldn't just run off at first sight of me being alone. I waited for a while until he finally showed up.

"Hey there, Kyle, where is John? Is he in the bathroom or something?" Coach Stally asked politely as he scanned the restaurant looking for Mr. Robinson.

"I'm sorry, sir, but he couldn't make it. Something had come up. He thought it would be okay for me to go alone. That way you wouldn't have been stood up." I can't believe I had just told a lie. This couldn't go on for too long before it gets back to Mr. Robinson. I honestly don't think he will be too thrilled once he becomes aware of my actions. The deeper I was getting the sicker I was feeling. I just couldn't ignore the fact that I was getting closer to solving this mysterious relationship between Jo Anna Kilo and Mr. Robinson.

Coach Stally proceeded to seat himself and look through the menu. Things were quiet for a moment while he and I both scanned our menus until he finally placed his on the table and spoke. "John doesn't really know you are here, does he?" Coach Stally was staring across the table into my soul. I could tell he wasn't too thrilled in being played to come meet me alone. Surely he assumed my intentions couldn't have been good. "What is it that you are up to, Kyle? Why would you set up such a meeting? What is it that you are searching for that John hasn't told you already?" I could tell by the tone of his voice, he was demanding an answer for some clarity on such a set up.

"I'm sorry, Coach Stally. I couldn't help the curiosity of wanting to know more about Mr. Robinson's relationship with Jo Anna Kilo. It seems to be a touchy subject to him. He has been acting strange ever since we last visited the college. He had never even spoken her name until then. I am so caught up in wondering why and how he could be so affected by old memories of her." I had come clean. Hopefully Coach Stally would have enough mercy on me to give me a little insight on the whole ordeal.

"Well, I'm sure he has told you as much as she broke his heart after he could no longer play basketball?"

"Yes, sir, I am well aware of his knee injury that ended his career. He had just never told me that he had a girlfriend at the time that wouldn't settle down with him because she wanted to pursue her own dreams of becoming a basketball star." Coach Stally began to have a blank stare after hearing the story I told him. There was a brief moment of silence before he stood to his feet.

"Well, then there you have it, Kyle. If that's what he told you then why are looking for anything further than that? Surely you weren't hoping that I would tell you a different story than what John had told you? Son, I don't condone what you are doing to my friend. I will do this much for the sake of you two and your relationship together. I won't tell him that we ever met today. I suggest you drop what you're doing before you cause trouble between you and John. It was nice to see you again, Kyle. You've grown to be a fine young man. John is a wonderful guy, whom I admire most of all men. He has always put others before himself. Some people can be selfish in this world. John Robinson isn't one of them. Give him the respect he deserves. If he doesn't want to talk about Jo Anna Kilo, then respect that. You have yourself a good day, Kyle." Coach Stally turned and started walking away before I could utter another word. He was right. It was a disrespectful thing I was doing. I shouldn't have went snooping behind his back and treating him like a liar. I sat there in the restaurant for a while drinking water after water in deep thought. I thought of how shameful it was of me to have gone this far. Even though Coach Stally said that he wouldn't say anything to Mr. Robinson, it would still be difficult to look him in the eyes knowing all that I have done up until now. Surely I can find some way to apologize and smooth it over with him.

It was a long ride home as I thought about the meeting between Coach Stally and myself. I felt awful. I didn't know how I was going to smooth things over with Mr. Robinson. I couldn't even fathom how I was even going to bring this up to Mr. Robinson. All I know is this could not go over well with him once I bring it up. Other than that, I couldn't get the reaction Coach Stally gave me out of my mind once I had told him the story that Mr. Robinson had told me. Something still seemed off about the whole situation. Maybe he was mad because how I set him up and was going behind Mr. Robinson's back with the whole Jo Anna Kilo story. He was right about me being disrespectful, but his response I couldn't quit replaying in my head. I had finally gotten home. I went straight to my study, lit the fire place, poured myself a drink and went through some old photos of me and Mr. Robinson before I decided to go to bed for the night.

I had so much on my mind last night. I really couldn't find the time to focus on anything else. All I could do was focus on what a fool I have made of myself. As I woke up this morning I felt distant from the world. I didn't want to face anybody at work knowing what I had done. How could I face Mr. Robinson? Mother certainly will not approve of what I had done by meeting Coach Stally behind Mr.

Robinson's back. Sooner or later, I would have to face the music. Everything was slow this morning from the time I got out of bed. I had no zeal or inspiration for going about my day. This morning's shower was slow. Breakfast didn't taste the same. I didn't put much time in my appearance. The drive to work was slow. I was dragging in the front door of the nursing home. I didn't want to be there or anywhere where I could be approached by my mother or Mr. Robinson. I really wanted to get it all out and move on but I didn't know where to start. It all started with that stupid trip and that stupid photo album. If I had known about Jo Anna Kilo then I wouldn't be so adamant about trying to get to bottom of this story. Was Mr. Robinson telling me the truth? Was that the whole story that he told me? Part of me deep down inside feels like there is more that he isn't telling me. The other part of me feels like a jerk for accusing him of not telling me the whole story. I was in limbo on what to believe and what not to believe. As I thought about it, things were just getting worse. If he was lying about the story; made me wonder if Mother was lying on her part also? Were they both lying or did mother know nothing more than what she had told me?

I wanted to talk to someone but who was I to talk to? I didn't want to bother Kira with the whole story on top of what she had going on. I don't think that my friends could be much of any help. The only ones that could bring clarity to the whole situation were my mother and Mr. Robinson.

I eventually mustered up the nerve to go visit my mother. I merely just walked in her quarters and sat in the recliner. I didn't even say a word upon entering her room. I just sat there staring at a photo album on the coffee table. I sat there staring at that photo album thinking about the photo album that he was hiding from me. I wanted to see that one. No other photo album at this moment mattered more than the one that I had not seen in his office. Should I break in his office and pry it from the locked drawer in his desk?

"Hi, dear, I don't even think I heard you come in? How long have you been sitting here? What is the matter? Is it Kira and her father?" Mother had interrupted my thoughts once she entered the living room. It was blatantly obvious I wasn't being myself today.

"No, Mother, it's nothing like that. It's that photo album. I can't get my mind off the thoughts of what might be in that album. I can't stop thinking that there is more to the story. I feel like Mr. Robinson isn't telling me the whole truth. I don't know if what he is struggling with is in that album or is he struggling with the whole story about Jo Anna Kilo? How did he seem yesterday on the little outing that you guys had gone on?" I wanted to know if he was displaying the same behavior with mother or was it just with me.

"He seemed fine yesterday. We talked about various things, but he never seemed like he was troubled about anything. Can I ask why this is so important to you dear? What if there was something he was hiding or wanting to tell you? Once you have gotten to the bottom of the story by forcing him to tell you anything ahead of time until he might be ready; would that make you feel any better? I'm not saying that he is hiding anything. I am just trying to figure all of this out and why you are obsessed with the whole Jo Anna Kilo issue. It is obvious that no one has given her a second thought but you. She may not be all that important if John hasn't ever mentioned her name to you."

"It's okay, Mrs. Brenda!" Mother was interrupted by a voice behind us. I knew that voice. The sound of that voice sent chills down my spine. The sound of that voice traveling through my ears left me immobile. That voice was so familiar to me. It was Mr. Robinson. I immediately became sick to my stomach.

He entered the living room. I never turned my head to make eye contact with him. The whole time he entered the living room; all I could think about was how long had he been standing there listening to our conversation. Before I knew it, he was standing in front of me looking at me as I sat there in the chair. Once I looked back at him, I noticed he had the album tucked under his left arm. The pit in my stomach had gotten deeper. The knot in my throat swelled as the moment continued to climax.

"Oh my God, John, I don't know if..." Mother's eyes began to swell up with tears. She was speechless as she looked up at him. I could tell that something was wrong. I could tell that she recognized that photo album. She knew more about that album than she had led me to believe.

Mr. Robinson looked back at her and tears began to form in his eyes as well. "It's killing me, Mr. Brenda. He needs to know so he can move on. He needs to know so we can all move on. Kyle, I had a missed call from Coach Stally yesterday. The voicemail had said that he was outside the restaurant looking for my truck but didn't know if I had ridden with you or not. The whole thing had caught me by surprise. I called him back. He and I had a long talk on the phone about what had went on yesterday in the restaurant. He said you were concerned about me and how I had been behaving after we left the school. The other day you stopped by and I was looking over this photo album. I was wondering when would ever be the right time to show you this photo album. The truth is that there will never be a right time. The truth is that there will only be time." He looked over to mother, then he placed the photo album in my lap. I had become nauseated. I couldn't even bring myself to open it at a first. I had been so adamant about getting my hands on it. I had put so much thought into how I would, and now it is being handed over to me to look at. Deep down, I knew and didn't know what to expect if I had opened it. I thought I would feel better once this moment arrived. I thought I would feel clarity. I was vigorously searching for answers. I was relentless at getting to the bottom of everything. Now I didn't even want to experience what was going on at the moment. I knew that things were about to change from this moment on. Life was going to take a turn. It was just undetermined on which way life was going to turn. I then opened the album. It was full of Jo Anna Kilo and Mr. Robinson as I suspected. As I progressed through the album, my stomach began to turn with every turn of the page. The more I turned, the more Jo Anna Kilo's stomach began to swell. She was pregnant! The last fifty percent of the photo albums pages were blank. I couldn't cry. I couldn't even speak. All I could do was stare at the blank pages and keep turning.

Then tears began to fall on the album and I felt Mr. Robinson's hand on my shoulder. "Son, I am sorry for all that has been going on. It's just that I didn't ever want to alter the way things were or have been. Your life seemed to be going so well up until you met Kira and started feeling alone and left out. Then I realized that a part of you felt empty. I wanted to help, but I just didn't know how. I was going to show you this album the day you found me looking through it. I just didn't know how. I knew things would never be the same between us afterward." I looked at Mother, and she was in tears. Her hands were folded her lap. I hadn't seen so much pain on her face since my father had passed. Wow, my father, or was this my father standing her in front of me? Or was that even me in her stomach? Part of me wanted it to be and part of me was hoping he would tell me that it was some other child she had aborted. My emotions were in an unstoppable whirlwind. I couldn't come up with the right question to ask as Mr. Robinson began to speak again. "She and I were very much in love Kyle. I thought it would last forever. She became pregnant her last year in college. The bigger he stomach grew, the farther apart I began to feel us grow. Jo Anna nor myself, believed in having an abortion. Off and on, she would go into these depressions and rants about how her career was over. She said she wasn't ready to be a mother. The day she went into labor was the turning point of everything. She had been planning to give you up for adoption. It was an idea developed between her and her parents. The agency and a lawyer were there present at the hospital. Everybody treated me as an outcast. After you were delivered, the agency had made an attempt to take you. Once I saw them trying to take you, I lost it. All I could remember was striking her father and shoving the case worker to the floor. The next thing I knew, I was on the doorstep of the nursing home with you in my arms. I was in such shock. The police came to the nursing home and arrested me for shoving the case worker. Mrs. Brenda and Kenneth watched over you while I stayed in jail for a couple of days. Jo Anna had signed you over to the agency before you were born. There was already a family picked out. Not once did she ever tell me about any of her plans. The authorities told the McCormics about all that was going on. Kenneth had contacted a lawyer and the intended family. They had agreed to return the legal rights over to me as the father, but I was unstable. Mrs. Brenda had been watching you the whole time while I was in jail and going to court for the assault on Jo Anna's father and the case worker.

Eventually, all charges were dropped and custodial rights were given to the McCormics. I was in no shape to take care of you Kyle. For the first five years of your life, I had to see a therapist. The McCormics took care of everything while I was getting help and going to school. By the time I had gotten my life together for you to be with me, I had noticed you were already looking at the McCormics as your mother and father. I didn't want to ruin that for you. I didn't want to make things confusing for you or cause you any pain. So I got everything in order and stayed as close as I possibly could. They never denied me my fatherly duties. I taught you all that I knew. I never missed Christmas, birthdays, school events, or anything that you were involved in. I always hoped that one day you would become a man, so we could have that special talk, and you might forgive me for all that you had been through. The right time never came because I was so afraid that you would hate me for the rest of our lives. I had contacted Jo Anna once while you were in middle school. I was hoping she had a change of heart, but she said for me to never contact her again. She changed her number and later her address changed. That night at the college, Coach Stally asked me if you were aware of all that had happened. I told him that you haven't been told yet, but I was getting around to it. I asked him did he know of Jo Anna's whereabouts, but nobody knows where she is. I'm sorry it came to this, Kyle. I never meant to hurt you or for you to be hurt." I sat there in silence trying to process everything that he was saying. I couldn't believe how this was unfolding. How could no one tell me and continue to live a lie the whole time? How could mother or Mrs. Brenda let this go on and on? Who ever considered the damage this would cause?

I looked at them both and couldn't find the words to say. I simply placed the album on the coffee table and walked out of the room. I could hear Mrs. Brenda or my mother crying hopelessly as I was exiting. I didn't even stop by my office to grab my things. I walked straight out the front door, hopped in my car and drove straight home.

I had taken a bottle of wine and sat in the living. I sat there staring off into the flames, thinking and drinking in complete silence. All I could hear was the crackle from the fire and my thoughts playing over and over in my head. Thirty-five years of living this lie. Thirty five years of my real father allowing someone else to take his place as Dad in my life. Thirty-five years of watching me grow up and saying nothing. I even thought about how I felt a while back about being alone and wondering who my parents are. Mother or Mrs. Brenda knew the whole time while she was trying to comfort me with her advice. The two people I trusted with all my thoughts and all my secrets knew the whole time. All this time, they had the answers. The tears of Mrs. McCormic and Mr. Robinson never evaded my memory. I couldn't help the pain I felt at how broken she looked as the truth was spilling out into reality. Who was her heart breaking for, me or Mr. Robinson? Maybe she was torn because she had come to the realization of her living a lie all of these years. My love for both of them overrode the hatred and anger I wanted to feel for them. Jo Anna Kilo was obviously the one who truly abandoned me. I had been so adamant in tracking her down up until this point.

At this point, I had no desire to even want to meet her or give her a second thought. The only person I had left to trust and talk to was Kira, but she had her own thing going on with her daughter. Then it made me think of her father. My issues grew as I added the ignorance he displayed that day out in front of the pharmacy. I sat there all night thinking and drinking. Wine wasn't relieving any of the pain so I went and retrieved something stronger from the study. There on the couch I sat all night long teetering back and forth between sorrow and anger. I was angry, but I could still feel the pain both of them were feeling knowing that the truth would hurt. Deep down, I knew they had done the best they could with the situation they were facing. All the talks mother and Mr. Robinson had about Kira's situation had filtered over into my own. The talk that Kira and I had that day as we toured the nursing home had started to come to mind. All the advice I had been receiving for someone else was preparing me for this inevitable moment in my life. I stayed up all night drinking until I passed out in the living room on the couch.

CHAPTER THIRTEEN

I woke up the next day on the couch. When I looked at my watch, I noticed it was already noon. I could hear my alarm blaring upstairs in my room. I got up to pour out the rest of my glass in the sink. I picked up my cell phone off the island in the kitchen. I noticed I had several missed calls and three voicemails. The first one was from Mrs. Sharon. She had called once she had noticed my folder was stilling lying on her desk. After I heard her message, I called the nursing home to call in a personal day. After I called in to work, I went back to my voice messages. The second message was from Mr. Robinson and the third was from mother. At this point, I wasn't ready to face them or anybody else. A rock had been dropped on my chest. I felt like the world stopped spinning and time stopped ticking. I couldn't find it in me to be too concerned with anything else, and the alarm was still blaring upstairs. I went to the downstairs bathroom and turned on the shower; alarm was still blaring upstairs. I felt like a zombie. I felt like the life had just been sucked out of me. I thought to myself, *I don't call in.* Rarely have I ever called in. It was my routine to visit mother every day. I didn't want to face her. What could I say? What was there to say? To me the woman that I loved and admired more than anyone on the planet was lying to me the whole time. My father was playing my best friend while I was being raised by someone else. The whole time that all of this was going on nobody ever thought to just tell the truth. At this point, I couldn't tell which was better. Would I have really wanted to hear the truth? "Hey, Kyle, your mother gave you up for adoption because she wanted to pursue her career in basketball. Your father couldn't care for you because

143

he was a basket case. The only people to care for you, is this rich white couple that specializes in the care of poor pitiful black folk." My heart hurt because I knew it wasn't true, but I was so angry. I didn't know who to be angry at. Should I be mad at mother and Mr. Robinson? Should I be mad at myself? Had I not been so adamant about uncovering the truth about Jo Anna Kilo; things would have been completely normal. Was I better off not knowing the truth?

After I had gotten out of the shower, I had another missed call. It was Kira. She was calling to see if I had wanted to meet at Alice's Café in the next couple of hours. I didn't even bother returning her call. I was so deep in my feelings that I had no concern for anyone. I could care less if anyone left or stayed in my life. I finally turned off the alarm upstairs. My phone had rung for most of the day. Every time it rang, I would silence it and ignore whoever was calling. Mainly it was mother and Mr. Robinson. I saw where Kira had called a couple more times. I had even quit listening to my messages that everyone had left. All I had done for most of the day was sit on the couch, drinking and watching the fireplace. There were a few times I would go out back, stand on the deck, and gaze out into the field in deep thought for a moment. I knew before long, someone would eventually come looking for me. I called into work and put in vacation for the rest of the week. Before I knew it, the day had passed. I had never left the house. All I had eaten was a little bit of the left over spaghetti that Kira had fixed and left in the fridge. I was almost down to the last drop of whiskey. I was never a heavy drinker. I would have a little bit to drink from time to time. It's what my father would do. Before he would retire to bed, he would have a small sip of whiskey to help him relax. It was just a habit I had picked up from who I knew wasn't my father but looked at as my father.

Mr. Robinson always preferred not to drink due to what he had experienced with his father. I had finished the bottle in the study where I would doze off for the rest of the night.

Instead of my alarm waking me up the next day, it was loud knocking at the door. Who could possibly be beating on my door this early in the morning? I still felt inebriated, and I reeked of alcohol. Whoever it was continued to knock from the time I woke up until I had gotten to the door to open it. It was Kira.

"Kyle McCormic, I have been calling you since yesterday." She walked straight past me into the house as she was fussing. She finally turned around to face me after she had gotten good into the house. "Oh my goodness, what happened? Have you been drinking? I mean, well, it's obvious by the look and smell of you." She looked me over and looked around the living room at the blanket and pillows on the floor in front of the couch.

"He's my father, Kira!"

"Who, who is your father?" I had completely forgotten that she had never met Mr. Robinson. I could remember talking to him about her, but I don't think I ever talked to her about him. I turned and walked over to the couch to sit down. She followed in behind me and sat down.

"Who is your father, Kyle?" she asked again as I was trying to gather my thoughts and think of how I would explain the story to her. She knew that the McCormics raised me and the fabricated story I told her about being abandoned.

"Remember the day you met my mother at the nursing home? Remember that story she had told you about me being abandoned? It was all a lie. It was all fabricated to hide what had truly happened, except for the abandoned part. I wasn't left on the back step in a suit case. I was brought there by my father. Well, the guy that was supposed to be my father, I guess. Mr. Robinson is a man that had been close to the McCormics since before I was born. He had problems with his family. His mother abandoned him and his father was an alcoholic. Too make a long story short, the McCormics took him in and helped him finish school and go to college. While he was off in college, he met a woman by the name of Jo Anna Kilo. The two played basketball for the men's and women's team at the college. They had a long relationship, but she eventually had gotten pregnant. She was more concerned about her career in basketball. So she gave me up for adoption without telling Mr. Robinson. Once he found out about it on the day of my birth, he got into a scuffle with her father and the case worker. He fled with me back home to the nursing home where he was trying to get help from my mother. He went to jail. They took me in and adopted me. That's the whole story in a nut shell. You were right in what you said, "How could anyone ever do such a thing without trying to keep a close eye on me?"

He was like my best friend when I was growing up. He would come get me and take me places. He taught me lots of things like how to ride a bike, sports, how to play chess, and so forth. He came to all my games and events. He was always there playing the role of a highly concerned or caring outsider. The whole time he was actually my biological father. Not once did he ever mention anything. He even lived the lie and told me he had a knee injury that ended his college career. I was the knee injury that ruined his career. How I found out is when he and I went to a college game at his old college. I took him there thinking that it would be a good idea for us two to hang out. We have always been close since I was child. We did things like this often. I didn't know it would lead to all of this. I discovered Jo Anna Kilo, my real mother, when I was looking at old photographs of him and her in a trophy case at the college. When I asked who she was, his whole demeanor changed. He had begun to act strange from that moment on. So I decided to do some digging on this Jo Anna Kilo. I pushed and pushed until it led me up to finding out a couple of days ago at the nursing home. I found out the day before yesterday he was my father. I found this out as he overheard a conversation between me and mother. I am sorry I didn't answer or return your calls. It was nothing personal. I just didn't want to be bothered with anybody due to all that was going on at the time. I feel so lost and confused between being hurt and being angry. The whole story sucks. I don't know what's better; being abandoned and not knowing who left you, or being abandoned and finding out whom it was that left you? I don't know who to be mad at. Should I be mad at Mr. Robinson for giving me up? Should I be mad my mother for aiding in the lie the whole time, or should I be mad at myself for pushing the issue? It seemed like everything you and I talked about at the nursing home that day has come into fruition." As I finished talking, I noticed the tears forming in Kira's eye.

"I am so sorry that things unfolded the way that they did Kyle. I'm happy that you found your biological father. I am happy to find out that at least one parent wanted you and stayed close by to make sure you were okay. I know it's hard to see right now, but they did what they had thought at the time was best to shield you away from the hurt and devastation that was going on at the moment. I believe they both love you and everybody did the best they could with the circumstances they were facing. The only problem I do have with the story is that it is similar to my situation. I want to tell Chelsie the truth, and I am sure that they both wanted to tell you the truth the whole time. They just didn't know how or couldn't find what they thought would be an easy enough time. I know this because it is the same thing that I am going through. The truth is there isn't an easier time. Seeing how you have responded scares me to the point of not even telling Chelsie. Seeing how angry and confused you are proves my father right. Things are better off this way. I would just make Chelsie angry at me and the rest of the family. She would push us all away like you did. She may even end up blaming herself and causing harm to herself, like you did. Maybe I shouldn't say anything." At that moment, my heart made its way into my throat. I was supposed to be in Kira's corner helping her get her daughter back the whole time. I had supposed to been encouraging her and setting somewhat of an example. The way I responded to my issue has brought discouragement to Kira in getting her daughter back. The whole time Kira was hoping that her daughter would receive her with open arms, but I had stolen that dream from her by what was going on in my life. I immediately started feeling selfish. I was speechless. Kira didn't say another word. She kissed me on the cheek and made her way out the door. I wanted to run and stop her, but I didn't have the words to say once I caught her. This whole thing has spun out into an awful mess. I doubt she will ever talk to me again.

I sat there for a while after she had left. I felt like I was in a nightmare that I could not wake up from. Everything had gotten worse for me in the matter of two days. I lost my mother, Mr. Robinson, and Kira. I was to the point where I didn't want to go back to work. I was to the point where I didn't care if I had a job or not. I didn't know if I would return to work after this vacation time was up. I felt like my life wasn't real the whole time. I wanted things to be different, but all sorts of past conversations started replaying in my head. The conversations and advice mother and Mr. Robinson would give. They were sitting me up the whole time to make things easier on themselves for the time when the truth would come out. What kind of sick and twisted game had they been playing with my mind? The more I thought about it, the more betrayed and tricked I felt. The more betrayed and tricked I felt, the more, bitter I had become.

I didn't have the energy to clean up or leave the house. I was napping and sleeping in various places around the house. I wasn't eating and the only fluids I had drank, was all the alcohol I could find around the house. Day after day, my sorrows were getting bigger. My pit was getting deeper. One moment I could think of Mother or Mr. Robinson, the next I would think about how I discouraged Kira.

Jacs would eventually call. She told me how mother had told Kevin about what had happened. Uncle Kevin had told Marcus, and that is how Jacs had found out. The guys would always send Jacs in their place when they wanted to help me with serious issues. She seemed to be the mediator and comforter out of the bunch. Guys aren't generally all that good at comforting other guys. She knew us and she knew how to get through to us. I told her what was going on and she had rushed over. I explained to her the whole story. Jacs said that she had suspected that Mr. Robinson could have been my dad. She said that he and I were alike in many different ways. She even made the joke that he and I have the same walk if you watched us walk side by side. She was happy that Mr. Robinson was my father. She always thought a lot of Mr. Robinson. She told me how worried the guys were. Jacs stayed for a while. She even helped me clean up the living room and the kitchen. She did most of the work, while I slow poked at it. After she had left, I continued to try to pick up. I needed to remove the essence of the last few days of not doing anything but leaving my mess and sorrow lying around the house. Before she left, she let me know that she and the guys were waiting on me to come around, and to call her if I needed anything.

I eventually called work and put in for another week of vacation. I was still undecided about keeping my job. All I know is that I wasn't ready to face mother or Mr. Robinson at the moment. I didn't hate them. I was just upset and angry. I needed to time to myself. I needed to process all that had happened and what was going on. Mr. Robinson and mother called every day. I never picked up, but I did start listening to the voice messages they would leave after every call. I was slowly gaining my energy back as I would do things around the house. I started a few projects around the house. The only time I would leave the house was to get material that I needed to complete my task. I hadn't heard from Kira, nor did I bother to call her. I assume she is done with me. I do hope that she finds the courage to tell Chelsie and work things out with her father. I know my hopes and my reaction didn't line up together, but it didn't change the way I felt about Kira in hopes of restoring things with her daughter. I knew that I would eventually talk to mother and Mr. Robinson again. I just wasn't sure on how things would be going forward. Would I continue to call her mother? Would I ever consider calling Mr. Robinson my dad? How was I to view and address him in the future? Was there any need to go visit mother every day? How was I to view them both?

CHAPTER FOURTEEN

A week had passed and I hadn't been out of the house except for my projects. I had painted the kitchen and the guest rooms, plus rearranged the furniture in the living room. I had gotten most of my energy back. I was on the last day of vacation before returning to work. I still wasn't sure on how I felt returning back to work or even continuing to work for the nursing home. I still had some discomfort and uncertainty on how to approach Mr. Robinson and how to get along with mother. The calls had stopped the last couple of days. I still hadn't heard from Kira. I assumed it was pretty much over and that I should just let it be. I couldn't handle her being so discouraged by me, and I'm sure I was not good company to her neither. I had gotten the house back in shape as far being clean.

On my last day, I decided that I would go out to the stores and do a little shopping. I hadn't really had a day to myself in a while. I couldn't remember the last time I went for a drive on my own, ate a nice restaurant, went to a movie, or shopping for some new clothes. It had finally dawned on me how routine my life had become. So I decided to have this last day to myself. The first thing I did was go to Alice's Café to have my favorite coconut mocha. I sat there in my favorite booth, enjoyed my favorite drink and did a little reading. After I left Alice's Café, I went to the mall. I piddled around in the department stores looking for a good buy on some clothes. It was about time for some new work clothes anyway. I had found some nice shirts and slacks on clearance. I ended up buying almost a week's worth of wear in one store. Once I had finished shopping, I had decided I would close out my day with a movie. I used to go the movies a lot when I was single. I remember when I had first started my job, I would go out to eat and to a movie every two weeks. It was my very own way of a treat to myself on every pay day. I was standing in front of the ticket window trying to select a film until I felt a tug at the tail of my coat.

"Hello, Mr. McCormic, what movie are you here to see?" The voice was so familiar. I knew who it was as I slowly turned to address the tug at my coat. I was right on the money. It was Kira. She was standing there with Chelsie.

"Hello, Kira! I don't know yet, I'm quiet undecided. What are you going to see? And you must be Chelsie." I turned and extended my hand to the young beautiful teenage girl accompanying her. "I have heard so many wonderful things about you. Kira talks about how close you two are and how much of a good time you guys always have. It is nice to finally meet you." I never forgotten the fact that Kira and I haven't talked in almost two weeks. I just didn't want to make things awkward in front of her "niece." They both seemed happy and I didn't want make anything else worse than it already has been.

She accepted my gesture and responded, "Yes, sir, Mom and I have always had fun together. She has always been there every step of the way. I don't know what I would do without her." I was devastated at the teenage girl's response. I was in shocked. I tried to replay what she said in my head without raising suspicion. I wasn't so sure if I had heard the girl correctly. Did she really call Kira mother? They both could obviously see the look of shock and confusion on my face.

"Mother," I couldn't say another word except for mother. Was Kira lying to me as well about her whole story? Did I hear the girl right?

"Yes, sir, she's my mother. I am so happy that she is and that I have her in my life." She was so happy and full of excitement at knowing that Kira was her mother. I just couldn't grasp how well this child was accepting Kira as her mother. I mean, did she not feel a certain way once she found out? Was there no anger at being lied to all of the past years? The questions started to just roll off in my head. I was in awe at how comfortable and excited she was to address Kira as her mother. "I was so excited to find out she was my actual mother. I enjoyed her as she was my Aunt Kira, but I used to wish she was my real mom so I didn't have to grow up without one. I had kind of suspected it at times on account of how loving and caring she was. I had always thought my suspicions were due to how much I had longed for a mother, and she was the closest one I had. I thank God that she is. It saddens me at what had happened to my mother to cause all of this debauchery, but I am glad things are finally in their proper arrangement." I was speechless as the little girl explained everything to me. Chelsie was happy to find out Kira was her mother. Chelsie wasn't angry at being lied to all of her life. It was amazing how she even showed sympathy for what had happened to her mother. I stood there stunned at all that was going on and being said before me.

"Chelsie, could you please give me a minute with Kyle? I think Meme and Papa are somewhere over in the lobby waiting for us to come out."

"Yes, ma'am, it was nice to finally meet you, Mr. McCormic." All I could do was smile at her in response as she departed from our presence.

You could see Kira's eyes watering as she looked into my eyes. "Everything is okay, Kyle. I just up and told her the next day after we had our talk. I picked her up from cheer practice, took her out to eat, and just come right out with it. We both just stood there in restaurant holding each other and crying. I explained to her why things were the way they were and what made everyone make the decisions that were made up to this point in life. I was for sure that she was going to hate me and never want to speak to me again. I just knew once I opened my mouth that things would change for the worst. After seeing how you reacted to the news of your father; I knew had come to the realization that there was never going to be any right time to tell Chelsie the truth. The reality of it is that there is only just time. We could spend more time living out a lie or living out the truth. I had taken a long drive after I left your house. I had decided that I would tell her no matter the consequences. I was ready to quit living like I was living. I was ready to accept the possibility of being an outcast as long as Chelsie knew her real mother lived and loved her more than life itself. I was willing to live with being pushed away by my father. I just didn't want her to be without her mother anymore. I was worried about my father and what he would think, but Chelsie told him everything was okay and she was happier with me being her mother. I truly thank God for how everything turned out. I just hope one day, you can find it in your heart to forgive your mother and Mr. Robinson."

Kira stepped forward and wrapped her arms around my neck, squeezing me tight. We shared a long hug for a moment. She kissed me on the cheek as she pulled away to leave. I was just speechless. I didn't want her to leave, but I didn't know how to make her stay. I just stood there and watched her walk away. I finally noticed Mr. Alexander watching her as she was approaching him. He and I made I contact. I turned my head, then, walked out of the moving theater. I wasn't able to watch a movie as I was processing all that I had just experienced a minute ago. I needed get home and get to myself. So many things were going through my mind at once.

Before I could get in my car, I was stopped again. "Kyle, wait a minute please? I would like to have a word with you before you leave if it is okay?" It was Mr. Alexander. He had followed me out in the parking lot. "Before you say anything; I want to apologize for my behavior the other day at the drugstore. I was wrong for how I spoke to you. I have never been one to experience interracial relationships. There has never been a couple in my family. I don't even recall knowing any couples. I was never raised that way, so I don't know how to respond to such a thing. I just don't want my daughter to struggle. She has been through enough. I couldn't bear her to have any more adversity in her life. Fathers are protective of their daughters. I failed once a long time ago. I vowed to never let that happen again. The truth is that I don't know how interracial couples work. What I do know is that my daughter loves you and you obviously love her. It took me a while to process that after that day at the drugstore. I thought about it over and over, until I had come to the conclusion that being white or black really didn't matter when you have a man standing in front of you fearlessly displaying his care and concern for your little girl. And that is the type of man I would want to have my daughter—no matter if he happens to be black or white. Love covers all of the other the stuff. So I would be truly grateful if you could find it in your heart to forgive me and accept my apology?" Mr. Alexander extended his hand, and we shook hands making amends right there in the parking lot. "If things are still good with you and Kira, then, they are good with me. Just know, that you are welcome at my home anytime son. As he was walking away, I could see Kira out front of the building watching us. Once Mr. Alexander returned to her, they engaged in a strong father-and-daughter hug. I could tell she was crying in his arms while they shared the moment outside of theater. I waived as I got in my car and drove out of the theater parking lot.

I thought about the whole episode as it replayed itself in my head. Everybody was so happy and forgiving. Things turned out better for the whole family once the truth had come out. I thought about how Chelsie had longed for a mother. She reminded me of myself and how I had begun to feel the day Kira meet my mother. I had longed for my parents. I had longed to know what had happened to them. I had felt alone. Chelsie had the same scenario with Kira as I did with Mr. Robinson. I never thought of how he has always been there and that he never left my side. I put him in Kira's shoes for a moment. It must have been hard on him to stand back and watch his son growing up and not knowing that he was his real father. Knowing the pain Kira was feeling; I started to imagine the pain that Mr. Robinson could have felt.

As I had gotten home, showered and ready for bed, I kept comparing Kira and Mr. Robinson's situation in my mind. I started to see things from another perspective. Anger and bitterness was leaving my heart. Forgiveness started to fill all the empty space that bitterness had left. I didn't know how to fix things, but I knew that I needed to talk to my mother and Mr. Robinson, my father. He had always been there. He was trying to be a father to me the whole time given the situation and circumstances he was faced with.

CHAPTER FIFTEEN

I didn't know how things would turn out today, but I woke up this morning with a new purpose in mind. I was determined to figure out how I would fix things and get us all back together. I didn't even know where to start, but today was the day to get the ball rolling. I wasn't sure where Kira and I stood. I just hope that time can put us back together. I really don't want to intrude on the newness of the mother and daughter relationship that she and Chelsie were enjoying. I figured I would give it some time and call her later in the week.

I grabbed my paperwork from Mrs. Sharon as I entered the building like always. I fixed me a cup of coffee and headed to my office to get my work finished. I did my best to get things in order in a hurry. I couldn't really concentrate on what I was doing for thinking of all that had to be done concerning mother, Mr. Robinson, and myself. I rolled around different scenarios and approaches all morning long until I just left my office and headed to mother's quarters.

"Knock, knock, are you here?" I tried to enter the same way that I always have to smooth things over. Mother slowly walked out from her bedroom. She stopped and paused for a moment as she looked at me. I could tell she had been upset. The look on her face was as if one didn't know how to engage. "It's I mother. I know we haven't talked in a while, and I know I have hurt you by not responding or returning any of your calls. I am sorry for the pain that I have caused you. I just needed some time. Everything happened so fast and all at once. I didn't mean to hurt anybody. The whole time I was concerned with what was going on with Mr. Robinson and Jo Anna Kilo; I never thought for once that they were my biological parents.

The thought never once crossed my mind that they would end up being my parents at the end of all this mess, but that's all in the past now. I still want you to be my mother. I love you and I am grateful that no matter how things happened; God placed me in the care of wonderful people who did love and care for me. It doesn't matter what color you are or what color I am. All that matters is that we all love one another. Mother, I am so sorry." I could notice the tears rolling down her face as she slowly walked toward. I opened my arms and pulled her in as tight as I could. I had my mother back. I can only imagine the pain she had been feeling as she hadn't heard from me in the last week. She just stood there in my arms for the moment.

"I love you, Kyle Lucas. Nothing will ever change that. I never meant for you to be hurt. I just wanted you to be loved and feel loved. Maybe we should have told you the truth. I truly don't know. I just hope we all can move forward as a family. I hope none of this has changed the relationship we once had."

"Nothing will change our relationship, Mother. If anything, all this will make things stronger for all of us. I just have one huge mess to clean up. I still have to talk to Mr. Robinson. Is he here today?"

"No. He took today off. Your silence had really broken his heart. He called me this morning and let me know that he wasn't going to be here. He did ask if you were here today. I told him that I hadn't heard from you nor has anyone seen you. He was having a rough time here at work. He said he was going to stay home for the day. I think you should go see him. I think it would be easier for you two to talk on neutral ground. This is no place for you two to have a heart to heart. Go see him at his house. At least you can have a comfortable place to hear his whole side of the story. He had been really trying to find a way to tell you these last few weeks. You just found out too soon. Get out here and go find him. Go to him now, dear!" She kissed me on my cheek and sent me on my way.

I told Mrs. Sharon that I would be leaving early and wouldn't be back for the rest of the day. I hopped in my car and headed over to Mr. Robinson's place. When I pulled in the driveway, I noticed the garage door was up. After I had gotten out of the vehicle, I went to the front door and rang the doorbell, but no one answered. I thought it was strange so tried to go in the house through the garage but that door was locked as well. As I sat there for a minute, I began to hear continuous thumps out back. I made my way around the house. There was Mr. Robinson in the backyard splitting wood. His back was to me. I really didn't know what to say. I just stood there for a moment. As he leaned over to pick up another piece of wood, he caught a glimpse of me standing there. He slowly stood upright, turned and faced me. For a brief moment, he was just as speechless as I. All we did was stare at each other for a minute, which seemed longer.

"How was your vacation?" Mr. Robinson had finally broken the silence.

I noticed he didn't end with calling me son like he normally does. For the first time I had realized why he was saying it all this time and what he had actually meant. He was addressing me in his own way of hoping to tell me one day. Before I answered, I made my way closed to him. We were standing face-to-face. "Whatever happened to calling me son, Dad?" Upon hearing those words out of my mouth, dropping the axe, he quickly reached out and gave me the biggest hug he has ever given me. Even after I called him Dad, I could feel the weight of the world lifted off my shoulders. Nothing else mattered anymore. I was no longer alone. I had my real father. I had him the whole time but now everything felt real. For the first time in my life, the world felt like it was revolving in the right direction. I wasn't on a deserted island. I wasn't feeling like I had been shipped off to some far country. I was in my father's arms. I was with my real dad. I never needed to be found all along. I was home. He had been close by, protecting me, and watching over me the whole time. All the times I felt he was somewhere far off unknown; he had been there the whole time. That one hug, that first hug from my real father changed my whole life." After we hugged, he and I headed into the house. He poured up two sodas and pulled out the chess board like he always did. We began to talk for the first time. I could tell he was his old self but even better now that the truth was out in the open. He even told me that there was no knee injury after all. He had chosen to quit school to try and take care of his son.

Never once again did I concern myself with Jo Anna Kilo. She did abandon me. I don't hold any bitterness toward her in my heart. I hope wherever she may be, she has found peace. One thing that I will give her credit for is that she led me to my father. We sat there and played chess, chitchatting for hours. Dad had a billion more stories to tell about his time being roommates with Coach Stally. It was a new breath of fresh air for the both of us. All the pieces seemed to be in the right place. I could now understand the excitement Chelsie displayed at the movie theater. Speaking of Chelsie, there was one more mess that needed cleaning up.

When I finally left dad's house, I had called my mother. I wanted to let her know how everything went. She and I talked on the phone the whole drive home and a little bit after I got in the door. She was truly happy for me and Mr. Robinson. She said that she wanted us over for breakfast tomorrow morning. After she and I had gotten off the phone, I called up Jacs and the guys. Nobody would allow me to tell them what had been going on over the phone. Everybody ended up pilling up at my place. Everyone was so happy for me. We ordered pizza and sat around the island in the kitchen reminiscing over the past experiences everybody had with Mr. Robinson. They were all excited about him being my father. Trenton said it all made a wonderful story that I should write about some day.

The next morning, I woke up to the sound of Mother and Mr. Robinson downstairs in the kitchen. I immediately got out of bed, got showered, put on my clothes, and headed down stairs for breakfast. "What had happened to having breakfast at your place mother?" I asked with laughter in my voice and a smile on my face.

"I had changed my mind, dear. I wanted to have breakfast where it all started as a family; this time with everything out in the open and everyone knowing who they are. We have a lot of memories and tradition here. I didn't want to miss out on this one. Kenneth and I talked about the day that everything would be revealed. This is exactly what we had hoped for. I hope he is hearing about it in heaven. I'm so grateful that we are a true family now. We always have been a family, but today, marks a new beginning." Mother was excited. It even seemed like she had more energy than before. It seemed like we all had come to life.

"I totally agree, Mrs. Brenda. I had been doing the best I could to be a father from a distance. The whole time there was a small piece of me left lifeless not being able to come forward with the truth. I was scared the outcome would be totally different from today. I didn't know what to do when you were born Kyle. I didn't have any money or direction. I wanted to get myself together so I could take care of you. The McCormics helped make all of that possible. Kenneth would let me vent at times about wishing things were different. After I would finish, he would even try to encourage me to tell you the truth. He said that he would do whatever it took to make every-body feel like a family. I just couldn't do it. I didn't want anything to interfere with your life as you were growing up. I couldn't imagine what I would do if you started to go into a depression or would start failing because of finding out what happened to you at an early age. So I continued to be there however I could be without blowing my cover. I knew that this day would eventually come. I just didn't know when. I have been preparing for this moment the past few weeks. I quit college because I didn't want you to grow up like I did. I didn't want you to grow up without a mother or father. For the first couple of years after you were born, I tried to keep in touch with Jo Anna. I would call her and send her pictures of you. Then one day she answered the phone and we had a conversation that would be our last. She told me to never call or contact her again. She said that she was moving on with her life. She said that she had met someone and she didn't want you and I to interfere with the opportunity she had. She changed her number and address. The last of the letters and pic-tures I had sent, had come back with an extra package. She had sent me everything that I had sent her. I thought she would eventually have a change of heart after some time had passed, but I had never heard from her again. That alone motivated me even more to get my life together for you. I was so determined to give you what I longed for and didn't have, a father. As you know, my father was a drunk. He never made any ball games, school events, and never really made an attempt to have any time of relationship with me. He always told me that he could have done more with his life if he hadn't had me. He told me that he would still be with my mother if I had never existed. I vowed early in my teenage years that if I ever had a child, I would never be like him."

I was grateful that things turned out the way they did. I had always wondered what it feel like if I were to ever meet any of my real parents. I didn't know how I would respond. I was always afraid it would be someone I didn't like or wished I had never met. I was grateful that it was Mr. Robinson. He was truly a father that I could be proud of and want to be around. I was glad that we didn't have any catching up to do. Only thing that changed was how I viewed him now; no longer a friend, but my father.

Once we had finished eating, we all left to go to the nursing home. Mrs. Sharon had heard the news from mother yesterday. The look on her face was full of happiness when we all had come through the door. She told us how happy she was to hear the news and glad that I had found my father. Mother and dad walked me to my office and then he walked her to her quarters. Today was off to a great start and things were surely to get better. I couldn't explain the feeling I was feeling. Life just seemed like it had more meaning. It seemed like everything I was doing had more purpose. I didn't want to ever lose this feeling.

After work was over, I went home and showered. As I was getting out of the shower, I could hear someone knocking at the door. I wrapped myself in my towel and dashed down the stairs still soaking wet. When I opened the door, Kira was standing there with a pizza.

"Is it okay if I come in and we talk?"

"Sure, come on in. I was just getting out of the shower. Let me run upstairs and throw on some clothes real quick. I will meet you in the kitchen. Make yourself at home. I am sure you know where everything is in the kitchen." I was interested in how this talk was going to go. I hope she had some good news and wasn't about to ruin a perfect day. I ran upstairs and threw on a T-shirt and some trunks. We both pulled up two stools, and sat next to each other at the island in the kitchen. She had already poured two sodas for me and her, while we were eating the pizza from the box.

"My father told me about how he apologized to you at the theater that night. Chelsie says that she likes you. Mother already likes you. So I am going to just come right out and say it. I love you Kyle and I don't want this to end between us. Now that everything is in place in my life, I want us to pursue this relationship to the next level. If you don't feel the same way or if this is a bad time, I understand. I know that you still have your issue with finding out who, your real father is. I want you to be able to have some time to heal. I want to be here for you like you were for me. All you have to do is let me know where we stand or where you see me as far as your life is concerned." I hadn't really talked to Kira since that day I had found out Mr. Robinson was my actual father. There was that night at the movie theater, but that didn't count much for talking. She didn't know that we all had made amends and were getting along fine now. She wasn't aware of how wonderful things were going. To hear her say that she loved me just put the final piece of the puzzle in place.

"Everything is fine now with Mr. Robinson and me. We are all happy. I was so angry and bitter at first. It was the look of excitement on Chelsie's face that made me think of how much better things could be. She made me look at things from another perspective. The next day after that night at the theater, I went to the nursing home and talked to my mother first. Mr. Robinson had called in, so I took the rest of the day off to visit him at his house. We had a long talk over a few games of chess. Like Chelsie, I was glad that Mr. Robinson was my dad. He and I kind of had the same issue that you and Chelsie had. Seeing how happy Chelsie and the rest of the family were, made me realize how things could actually be with my family. The whole time I tried to help you, I was in need of help myself. We both needed each other's help and support. Kira, I thought I had run you off after we talked that night. Not a day went by that I didn't think about you or wonder how you were. Not a day went by that I wasn't hoping that things were getting better for you and your family. I'm glad to hear that you still want us to pursue things further, so do I." Kira and I had finished eating. We stayed in the kitchen and talked a little bit more afterward before she left to go home. After she had gone, I had a small glass of wine as I reflected on how things how have unfolded. I was now looking forward to the future. Everything seemed brighter now. No more secrets and no more mysteries. I felt like we all were family. I felt like this family was growing into something more special than it already was. Many people have been in the situation that I had been in, but not many had the same outcome? God has truly blessed me by placing some extraordinary people in my life. I could have been bitter. I could have been angry at everyone. My actions could have very well changed the course of this family. My actions could have changed the course of my life for worse. I could only imagine what holding on to all that anger and bitterness could have done to me. Those two weeks I spent angry and alone were bad enough. If I had decided to hold a grudge, mother and Mr. Robinson would have been so torn by my anger. I'm glad that didn't happen. I'm glad that Mr. Alexander had opened his heart up to the possibility of Kira and I being together despite the color of our skin. People truly have the power to destroy and change the course of life. Bitterness and forgiveness are a choice. If you can choose either, then choose forgiveness. It wouldn't have affected mother and Mr. Robinson as much as it would have torn me apart. Love truly does conquer all obstacles. Love overrides color, sex, origin, what you've done, and where you've been. That's what this family has shown this town. I decided to call it a night after I had finished my glass. I was looking forward to going to work tomorrow and telling mother and Mr. Robinson about the good news between Kira and me.

CHAPTER SIXTEEN

I couldn't wait to get to work today and share all the good news with mother. I felt like I had rose out of bed a new man. Today seemed like I had more to live for than I did last week or years prior. Even Mrs. Sharon seemed happier this morning when I had gotten to work. All of the staff were stopping me and congratulating me. Everyone at the nursing home that had heard the news was so happy for me. I stopped by dad's office before I started my work. He wasn't in there, but the door was open. This was the first time that I had known him to leave his office door open since we have worked together. I decided to go in and take a look around. He had redecorated the place. There were pictures up of me and him all over the place. It was cool thing that he had done. I could tell that he was finally starting to live free. You could even feel the freedom in the atmosphere. I proceeded on down the hall to mother's quarters. When I arrived, she and dad were in there chitchatting over breakfast.

"Good morning, son!" Mr. Robinson was the first to greet me. I'm glad they were both here. I wanted them both to know how things had worked out between Kira and me.

"Well, family, there is something else that I want share with you. Kira came by the house last night. I hadn't talked to her since the night of the first day that I had found out all the family news. We had a pretty rough discussion, none too good for the situation that she was going through. I was pretty sure that my reaction to the news had discouraged her and run her off for good. She and I didn't talk for over a week. I had met them the night before I had come back to work. She and Chelsie were at the theater with her parents. She had finally decided to come out and tell Chelsie after we had talked. She said she was just ready for the truth to come out, no matter what the outcome was to be. The look of excitement on Chelsie's face and in her conversation about finding out is what pricked my heart to see our situation in a different light. Her father even apologized for all that went on at the pharmacy that day. He said that his home will always be open to the man that loves and cares for his daughter. To be honest, the guy didn't seem all that strange after all, but back to the subject. Kira and I decided last night that we would stay together and pursue things further."

"Kyle. That is wonderful news. I'm glad that everything worked out for you two," Mother replied as she grabbed my hand.

"Well, I reckon I will get to meet the girl someday soon, I hope. Seems as though, I'm the only one she hasn't met." You could hear the sarcasm in dad's voice as he went on and on about never meeting Kira.

After I had shared the news with them, I had left to go back to work. I was already running behind. They continued on talking after I had left the room. I figured I had better schedule everybody over to the house for a meet and greet. I wanted to have everyone over to celebrate the new direction that this family was headed in.

The day was almost over. As I was finishing up my work for the day, I heard a "code red" page across the intercom. All the staff was rushing to the east wing of the building. When I had arrived on the scene, I could only see the shoes of the individual lying on the floor. I became frozen in terror as I noticed they were Mr. Robinson's boots lying there on the floor, toes pointed to the ceiling. Mrs. Sharon grabbed me and pulled me in the next room.

"Don't look, Kyle, he is okay. He just passed out is what one of the staff said. We called the ambulance to be safe. He is lying there conscious and responding to all of the staff. Go grab his things for him and meet him at the hospital." I was petrified. A million scenarios were going through my head.

I immediately ran down to his office and grab his things. Mother was coming down the hall as I was leaving his office. She hadn't heard the news of what had happened. She noticed how shook up I was in the midst of me trying to explain and get his things together before I left for the hospital. She insisted that I take her with me. I told the front desk to sign her out for me as were rushing out the front entrance to my car. The ambulance had already loaded him up and left as we were getting ready to leave the nursing home. Mother placed her hand on my thigh as I drove us to the hospital. She started say a small prayer before we finally arrived at the hospital. Kira had called right as we had gotten out of the vehicle and was entering the hospital. I told her what was going and where we were before I had hung up. He had been checked in and the receptionist gave us his room number. When we made it to his room, he was lying in the bed flat on his back. He looked over at me and smiled as we entered the room.

"Hey, son, come on in. The doctor had just left before you two had come in." He seemed in good spirits, but also a little worried.

"What did he say?"

"They ran some test and took some blood once I arrived here. He hasn't gotten the results back yet. They said they were going to keep me overnight and that he should know something in the morning."

I had gotten mother seated in the recliner over in the corner. I pulled up a chair next Mr. Robinson's hospital bed. "What had happened, Dad?"

"Tyler and I were changing out the bulbs in the fixtures of the main hallway. The next thing I knew, I was on the floor and everybody was standing over me. Tyler told Mrs. Sharon that I had passed out and fell off the ladder. He called the code as soon as he had gotten to me. I imagine that must have scared the poor kid. It is his first week on the job. One minute I felt fine and the next I'm laying here in the hospital. I just hope everything is all right." You could tell that he was worried after he finished his last sentence. I was worried for him as well.

"Hello, am I interrupting?" There was a knock on the open door. I turned to look over my left shoulder to see who it was. It was Kira. "I headed out the door and rushed down here as soon you and I hung up the phone. Hello, Mr. Robinson. My name is Kira. I'm

Kyle's girlfriend." Dad reached up and shook her hand as she introduced herself.

"It's finally nice to meet you. Kyle talks about you all the time. As a matter of fact, he can't quit talking about you. Seems that all he knows here lately is Kira." Even mother got a good laugh out of dad being so silly.

We all stayed there in the room with Mr. Robinson for the rest of the night. He and Kira talked for pretty much most of the night. Kira and I stepped out a little bit. We left to get everybody something to eat from an all-night diner down the street from the hospital. The hospital staff brought in more pillows, blankets, and an extra recliner for one of us to sleep in. I gave it to Kira while I stayed in the chair by dad's bed.

Early the next morning we were all awaken by the doctor entering the room. He introduced himself to the family before he began to speak to Dad. He told us that it was still unclear to why Mr. Robinson had passed out, but they had found cancer in his lung. He said that it was treatable as long as they hadn't found any elsewhere. Mother immediately covered her mouth. I could see the devastating look on her face. Father had died from cancer. Mr. Robinson sunk in the bed. The look on his face was hopeless. Someone may as well have tied a rock to his ankle and dropped him in the ocean. The doctor said they wanted to run more test and he would be free to go after they had finished. He wanted to prepare dad for treatment as soon as he could. I must admit that I was devastated at the news as well. I had determined in my heart that I would take him to every treatment and be there every step of the way. I even offered dad to stay at the house while he was going through all of this. That way he wouldn't be alone by himself. He insisted on staying at his home. Kira even volunteered to stop by and check on him from time to time.

Kira elected to take mother back to the nursing home while I stayed with dad. Mother loved the thought of them getting a little time together. She hadn't talked to Kira since the wedding. Mr. Robinson and I sat there and talked while the nurses came in and out of the room. We sat there for a few more hours until he was finally released. I drove him home. Once we got there, he poured two sodas and pulled out the old chess board. We played a few games and talked. We later went into the living room and found a couple of movies to watch on the television. He eventually fell asleep for a little nap in his recliner. I went out back and split some wood while he slept. I wanted some time alone to clear my thoughts and pray. I spent the day there. We left and ate dinner at Alice's, then came back and sat around the house for the rest of the day until I we both fell asleep in the living room.

I got up early the next morning to go home and get ready for work. Mr. Robinson said that he would be taking the day off. He said that he wanted some time alone to think and read up on his treatment from the brochures that he had gotten from the hospital. I was worried about him. He wasn't alone in this battle. This affected everybody. Especially now that things have changed for the better, this was the last thing that he needed to hear. All I knew is that I was going to be there every step of the way, no matter what the outcome was.

You could tell that Mr. Robinson's incident affected everybody at the nursing home. All the staff was so dry and quiet. Tyler stopped by my office to ask how he was doing and if he would be okay. I told him what the doctor had said and our plans going forward concerning Mr. Robinson. He said that he and his family would continue to pray for him. I remembered when Tyler was a teenager playing for the Highland basketball team. He and his family attended the same church that we did. He was a good kid. He got caught up hanging out with a bad crowd. He lost his scholarship to college due to drug addiction. After he had gotten cleaned up and been sober for some while, Mr. Robinson offered him a job on the staff.

At lunch, Kira stopped by and brought lunch. We took it down to mother's quarters so we could all sit down and chitchat. Mother was glad to see us both and have lunch with us. She tickled us both as she reminded us of the first time that she and Kira had met. She had me crying laughing as she imitated the look on my face as Kira was standing there looking at me with a puzzling look on her face as well. It was a good time. We had a good lunch as everyone tried their best to keep our minds off what was going on with Mr. Robinson.

After lunch, Kira and I took a walk around the facility. I introduced her to Mrs. Sharon and some of the staff. She seemed to never meet a stranger and everyone received her well. Before she left, she said that she would meet me at the house when I got off work. She didn't want me to be alone with all that was on my mind. I did feel better knowing that she would be there for me. I gave her a spare key that I had on my key ring, so she could let herself if she had gotten there before I did.

The rest of the day pretty much flew by. I made my way over to see dad at his house after I left work. I had brought him some key lime pie from the nursing home cafeteria. I figured he would like that since it was his favorite dessert that they served. Mine was the lemon ice box. We sat there and ate our slices for a little bit. I asked him about how his day had gone. He said that he had felt a little more confident after reading the brochures from the hospital. His confidence kind of put my nerves at ease as well. I really didn't want to leave him alone. I offered once again for him to come and stay with me at the house, but he insisted on time to himself.

When I pulled up in my driveway, I saw Kira's car. She greeted me as I entered the house. "Hey, sweetie! I figured you wouldn't feel like doing too much, so I brought pizza. I thought we could eat pizza and watch a movie or two."

"Yeah, that'll be fine, I reckon." I responded kind of dry. She could tell that I wasn't in the best of spirits. I kept saying to myself that I felt confident that everything was going to be all right, but I couldn't get my heart in line with my confidence. I just kept thinking; what if he doesn't pull through this? What if I lose my father right after I have just found him? I kept trying to tell myself that I had always had him in my life. I just hadn't had him as a father. Though I did and didn't know it, but it wasn't the same as knowing. As I stood there in front of Kira in the kitchen; the thoughts kept rolling around in my mind. I just started to break down and cry right there in front of her. I didn't say a word. All I could do was cry. I reached out, grabbed a stool to sit down, and Kira pulled me into her bosom as my tears began to flood the T-shirt of mine that she was wearing.

"I know it hurts, Kyle. I know it's not easy to go through. It's okay to lean on me. You're not alone in this. We all are hurting with you. We just have to pray and believe that everything will work out fine." Her words were comforting but still couldn't sooth the pain that I was feeling. I sat there and cried for a moment before I went upstairs and took a shower. After I had gotten cleaned up; Kira and I ate pizza and watched TV. She selected a few comedy shows. After all, I did need a good laugh.

CHAPTER SEVENTEEN

The following week, dad had begun treatment. The doctor had decided that surgery would fix the issue, but wanted to treat Dad up until the surgery. We had plenty of time together and catching up as Dad went through those few weeks of treatment. Kira would stay at the house off and on. Mother would stay once a week. Jacs and Marcus would stop by every once in a while to check on me and keep me company. I would go over to dad's house every day after work. We went out to dinner a couple of times, but most of the time we stayed home. With all that was going on; no one felt like doing much of anything. I would go hang out with him for a couple of hours to try and keep him in good spirits.

The day of the surgery, everyone was there. Even Mrs. Sharon was there. We all gathered around Mr. Robinson and prayed for him before they took him back. We all sat in the waiting area after they had taken him in to surgery. We all sat in the waiting area laughing and telling stories. Everyone that came in the waiting area ended up listening in, and laughing with us. I couldn't tell you how long the surgery had taken, but it felt like hours before we had heard from the doctor.

Everyone was silenced as the doctor approached me in the waiting area. He had said that Mr. Robinson was out of surgery. The procedure didn't go quite as he expected. Once they had opened him up, they had found more cancer. He said that they must have missed it somehow. I felt like I was in one of those movies like you see on TV when the doctor comes in with the bad news. I dropped to my chair right there as everyone gathered around me in silence. He said that they had told Mr. Robinson already. He said that Mr. Robinson only was allowing me and mother to come back to see him at the moment. The pit in my stomach was so large; you would think that it had to be surgically removed. Everyone went home but Kira. She decided to stay in the lobby and wait for us as we went in to see Dad.

I was speechless. Mother kept trying to comfort me as she was trying to keep it together as well. There wasn't much said in the room as we sat there with Mr. Robinson in devastation. He was just ready to go home and I was too. I couldn't believe this was happening to me. I couldn't believe this was happening to him. I couldn't believe this was happening to us. How could such a thing happen after I had just found my father? I thought to myself, "How could God allow this to happen?" Why would he allow all of this to happen after we had just now become a family? I wasn't ready for the road ahead. I wasn't ready to let go of my father. The doctor said that he wouldn't have long. He said that it was a matter of time in itself.

Mr. Robinson had elected to undergo no more treatment. I couldn't make of why he wouldn't. I couldn't understand why he would give up on us. Why wouldn't he take the treatment and hope for the best. I thought to myself that I would talk to him about it later on. I really hoped he would change his mind before the talk. I didn't want to say anything that could stir up a fight or cause an argument. All I knew is that I wasn't ready to lose my father after our relationship had been restored.

Mother elected to stay with Mr. Robinson after we left from the hospital. He said that he would like that as well. She wanted to stop by the nursing home and pick up a few things before we dropped them off at Mr. Robinson's house. Kira and I went back to the house. I wanted her there, but I wanted some time to myself also. She stayed at the house as I sat in the study. She would come in and check on me, but she did give me some time to myself.

Pretty soon winter was over. Spring and summer had flown by. It was winter again and Mr. Robinson had passed away. We were all gathered at my house getting ready for the funeral. I had done my best to prepare for this day, but yet, I still wasn't ready. I didn't even feel like getting dressed. I was willing to just go to the funeral in my pajamas. Kira and I were in my room. She was helping me get my tie together before we headed down stairs to get in the limousine.

"I've got it, Kira. Let me fix it for him?" Mother had come in to help. Kira moved out of the way and mother stood in front of me tying my tie around my neck. You could see tears forming in her eyes. "I wanted to do this one more time. I tied your tie when Kenneth passed. For some reason, I wouldn't feel right if I didn't this time." I knew what she had meant. She tied my tie when my father had passed. She wanted to tie my tie again, being that my father had passed. I understood. Once she finished tying it, she looked up at me and smiled. She placed her hand on my cheek and said, "You like just like your father". She then walked out of the room. I must admit that it felt good to hear that. Mr. Robinson was my father. I took once last look in the mirror, a deep breath, and headed downstairs to the limousine.

The ride over to the church was quiet. Mother and Kira planned the service. They had done a beautiful job. Everything was beautiful. The service was wonderful from the singing to the eulogy. The church was packed full of the town's people. Even Coach Stally and all the teammates showed up for the funeral. They had brought Mr. Robinson's jersey in a frame. It was up next to his casket amongst all the flowers and gifts people had sent. He had gifts all around the church. I was overwhelmed with all the love and care the town was showing for my dad. After we returned from the burial site, I met all kinds of people, as well as his old teammates as we all gathered to back at the church to eat. We had to load up Marcus's and Trenton's vehicles with all the gifts that were sent to take them back to the house. Mother, Kira, Chelsie, and Jacs arranged them all around the house once we got back. Mother was going to take some back to the nursing home with her as well. They all stayed for a while. I was ready for some time to myself. I was still a little numb from all that had happened and was going on. Kira was going to take Chelsie to her parents while I was going to take mother back to the nursing home.

She asked me to walk back to her room once we got there. Before we had gotten out of the car, I asked her for another piece of her advice. "Why would God do such a thing to me? Why would he take my dad away after I just had found him? Why would he take both of my dad's away with the same sickness?" I had a million questions that I felt no one would have the answers to. I was hoping mother had something soothing to say.

"Kenneth and I had this talk before he passed away. I asked him something similar. I asked him why God would take the love of my life away from me the way He was going to. Kenneth told me that God only receives those who pass away in this life. He doesn't take anyone away from us. Life happens to us all Kyle. The Bible says, 'I know the thoughts that I think toward you; thoughts of a future, hope, peace, and an expected end. We don't truly know why things like this happen in life. We just know that God is there to help guide us and comfort us through it all."

I liked Mother's advice on explaining the whole situation to me. It made more sense. I felt comfort in knowing that God welcomes those that believe to a better place. We got out of the car and entered the nursing home after she finished explaining things the best she could.

"I had finally finished my project that I was working on." She went back into her room to retrieve something. Out she came with this package wrapped in gift wrapping paper. "I want you to open it when you get home, dear." I didn't bother to ask her what it was. I just took it as she handed it to me and kissed me on my cheek.

Kira called to check on me as I was driving home. She was concerned if I was going to be okay. I told her that I would be fine. I wanted some time alone after all the company we had today. I didn't tell her about the package, but I wanted some time alone with it as well. She said that she would come in the morning for breakfast. I told her that would be fine.

Once I got home, I went into the study, lit the fire, poured myself a drink, put on an old record, sat down to open the package. It was a photo album. I recognized the album. It was the one mother had taken from the house last year. Underneath the album were some old photos and a lot that were taken in the past year. On top of it was an envelope. It was a letter from mother. "This is my greatest project ever put together. I knew one day you would find out the truth and meet your father. I just didn't know that things would turn out the way they did. John had begun to feel ill a few weeks before you found out he was your father. I urged him to see a doctor, but he insisted that he would be fine. He figured it was from his nerves of wanting to come clean in telling you the truth. He would come by and talk to me quite often. He didn't know how to tell you. He wanted to tell you, but was afraid you would be angry with him. Of course you know all of what I am saying in this letter. I wanted you to have something special in hopes to lighten things once he told you the truth. As you already know, things don't always turn out the way we had planned. He knew about this project and even supplied a lot of the photos and letters in this album. As you open it, you will see photos of you two from the time you were born up until now. Along with photos, there are letters throughout this album. He had written you letters throughout the years. It was his way of one day telling you the story and how he felt watching you grow and being involved in your life. I read them all. I hope you don't mind. Every letter brought tears to my eyes. I know you feel like you lost your father after you found each other, but the truth is, he has been there the whole time. I call it, the "McCormic Project." I placed the other photos in the box in hopes that you will continue these projects with your future family one day.

I sat up all night drinking, turning the pages and reading the letters. I could hear his voice in every last one of the letters I read. I started reminiscing from the past to this present day. The last photo in the album was one of Mother, Mr. Robinson, Kira, and me. I noticed Kira's beautiful smile in the photo and began to think back to the first night we met at the town high school rival football game. The letter attached to it was from Mr. Robinson. It read,

> I really enjoyed my last days on earth get-
> ting acquainted with my new future daughter-in-
> law and granddaughter. You are going to make a
> great father one day. I know things weren't as we
> wished they were between father and son, but I

hope I have been a better example to you then my father was to me. To hear you call me dad the past year bought back all the time that I had felt I had lost with you even though I didn't miss a moment. The whole time I longed for the day you would look at me as your father and I would be called "dad" by my son. I am so proud you and the man you have become Kyle. If you and I have learned anything in my passing, I hope it is love. Love is the most powerful weapon in the world. It overlooks all faults and offenses. Love has no color, race, or sex. It builds and lifts up. It strengthens and overcomes any obstacles we are faced with. That is what the McCormic/ Robinson family is all about. As you read these letters and review the photos, remember that I have loved you from the moment you came into this world. And as I leave this world, remember that I will always love you!

Love,
Your old man

About the Author

Storytelling and writing have always been a passion of mine. My Christian beliefs, studies of the Bible, and ministry experience make up the foundation of my writing. I think writing is one of the most powerful tools we have on this earth. I often refer to writing as a "superpower." Our words have the power to awaken, inspire, and change the perception of the reader for either good or bad. Writing can help us create a whole other alternate universe that opens our eyes and heart in the reality that we live in. Books take us on trips and journeys with the turn of every page. My ultimate goal is to touch and inspire people in places I may never go or experience!

CPSIA information can be obtained
at www.ICGtesting.com
Printed in the USA
LVHW090409180820
663426LV00002B/115